Means of Transit

Means of Transit

A Slightly Embellished Memoir

Teresa Miller

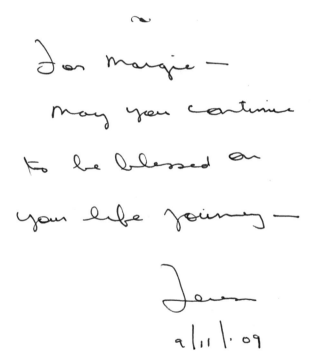

For Margie —
May you continue
to be blessed on
your life journey —

Teresa

9/11/.09

UNIVERSITY OF OKLAHOMA PRESS : NORMAN

Also by Teresa Miller

Remnants of Glory (New York, 1981)
Family Correspondence: A Novel (Tulsa, Okla., 2000)

Photographs are from the author's collection,
unless otherwise indicated.

Library of Congress Cataloging-in-Publication Data
Miller, Teresa.
Means of transit : a slightly embellished memoir / Teresa Miller.
  p. cm.
ISBN 978-0-8061-3971-5 (alk. paper)
1. Miller, Teresa. 2. Novelists, American—20th century—
Biography. I. Title.
PS3563.I42145Z46 2008
813'.54—dc22
[B]   2008014154

The paper in this book meets the guidelines for perma-
nence and durability of the Committee on Production
Guidelines for Book Longevity of the Council on Library
Resources, Inc. ∞
Copyright © 2008 by Teresa Miller. Published by the
University of Oklahoma Press, Norman, Publishing Divi-
sion of the University. Manufactured in the U.S.A.
1 2 3 4 5 6 7 8 9 10

In memory of Jean Crane Miller, who didn't get to make the journey with us

And for Jonathan and Isabel, artful travelers in their own right

Contents

Illustrations follow page 111.

Traveling Lightly in Familiar Territory

Recently there has been considerable debate about what constitutes memoir as opposed to autobiographical fiction. My own belief is that memoir, even as nonfiction, is open to literary license as long as it adheres to what many critics refer to as "essential truth." That truth, filtered through memory, is the basis for *Means of Transit*. In other words, this book isn't intended to be a chronological account of my life. Instead, it's a way for me to acknowledge a sequence of themes that are more relevant to my personal history than any experiences I can measure in calendar years.

Initially I'd hoped to discover a singular meaning to my story that might put it in a larger context. But that kind of self-knowledge continues to elude me, except for this new understanding—I came from a family that tried not to dwell on anything too unsettling. Just recently I realized the predilection in a literal way during an eleven-day power outage that left me at the mercy of a portable generator. As I told a friend, I felt like I was living in an RV that never went anywhere.

Yet this generator, which I regularly topped off with gas, fueled my television, phone, reading light—all those devices that transported me beyond the shadowy corners of my living room. I even assumed the demeanor of a weary tourist, making daily runs to the Shell station and visiting with strangers about how long a TV could run on a gallon of regular.

I've traveled these alternate routes before, flights of fancy as much as despair. And just as with other journeys that bridge great distances, they conjure up their own memories.

T.M.

Means of Transit

If her kiss
had left a longer weight upon my lips,
it might have steadied the uneasy breath,
and reconcil'd and fraterniz'd my soul
With the new order. As it was, indeed,
I felt a mother-want about the world,
And still went seeking.

—Elizabeth Barrett Browning, *Aurora Leigh*

W hen I was growing up in Tahlequah, Oklahoma, wondering how to get to bigger and more noteworthy places, my grandmother tried to teach me the essence of maps. "Traveling is a matter of heart, not miles," she'd remind me every time we set out in her '65 Buick. "Someday we'll visit about my journey to . . ." To hear Grandma tell it, she'd been around the world without ever leaving the Midwest, but when she spoke of London, she meant London, Arkansas.

I only halfway listened to Grandma's road talk, especially as I got older. Instead, I spent most of my time in the backseat with a Texaco atlas, looking for shortcuts to the starred cities that rated pages of their own. Chicago, Hollywood, New York—they were never on our itinerary, so I matched my fingertips to the atlas legend, counting off the miles to less exciting destinations.

"Let's not to wish our trips away," Grandma would caution, particularly when darker memories caught her off guard, causing her to falter at familiar crossings. Then I'd recall what the local women had told me in secret—how she'd overcome her bashfulness to bend down and kiss my mother in her casket.

But she hid her sadness well. Mostly I knew her as a relentless sightseer, who resorted to jingles of Oklahoma place-names to keep me entertained: "Sallisaw—Henrietta—Wagoner—Bushyhead." She'd traveled the same roads more than once in life, but she always expected our drives to be unforgettable—even if we were just crossing borders to pay our respects to old neighbors. "See that little clearing," she'd say, slowing down to tourist speed. "Grandpa and I once had a flat right about there, got into a fight, then made a picnic of it."

Only I wasn't interested in her flat-to-picnic philosophy—at least not yet. I was preoccupied with legends. So I'd bellow, "Five more miles to Little Rock," while Grandma roamed the countryside, looking for loved ones we'd left behind and consecrating her own landmarks.

Legends

My great-grandfather Mills traveled by horseback to
see the legendary actress Sarah Bernhardt perform
under a tent in Texas. Later describing the event as the
"experience of a lifetime," he spent his latter days be-
moaning the fact he could not swim. A self-proclaimed
theorist, he'd studied a journal article concluding that
swimming was an innate skill and convinced a group
of young men to throw him into a river so he could
reclaim his lost talent. But the currents were swift that
day, and it took twice as many men to save him. A few
years later, he died adrift in his easy chair, reading
aloud from the collected works of Shakespeare.

∽

I grew up wanting to be a dramatic actress—emphasis on *dramatic*—because I spent my formative years in front of the television, mesmerized by such high-powered, Kleenex-laden shows as *Queen for a Day, The Secret Storm,* and *The Edge of Night.* My father and grandparents were wonderfully progressive in that way, allowing my brother and me full access to uncensored TV. Not that they were negligent. They just felt that life itself had already placed too many restrictions on us.

The only series ever off-limits at Grandma Crane's house was *The Waltons.* Grandma believed that we were such a quirky family ourselves that tuning in to the well-balanced Walton clan might give us unrealistic expectations—and put undue pressure on our more eccentric relatives. She caught me mid-show one night, just as John Boy was telling his own grandmother that he wanted to be a writer. Dutifully I switched channels to *The Mod Squad,* and Grandma smiled with relief as I focused instead on a drug shakedown. "That's more like it," I could imagine her saying, as she pulled up a chair and watched with me.

But I'm leaping ahead of myself here, and a little desperately for I know full well that *The Waltons* didn't impact our relationship until later—after *Peyton Place* had been cancelled and we'd struggled through Alison MacKenzie's lingering coma. It's not that my memories are all that tricky. There's just this wildness, a reckless notion of eternity, that comes from conjuring up old dilemmas.

So suffice it to say that despite our differences, Grandma and I knew how to watch television together. In fact, one of my grandmother's ongoing concerns was that her other grandchildren, in "normal" family situations, didn't get to watch television often enough. We even enjoyed the advertisements, which gave us time to connect the storylines to our own lives, and we did so in perpetuity. Grandma, as she was quick to explain, would forever understand Constance MacKenzie—nothing was worse than having an ungrateful child or grandchild. And for my part, I could always relate to Allison's frustrations with small-town life. I wanted to get out of Peyton Place/Tahlequah, too.

As much as we identified with our favorite stars, we tried not to blur the often fuzzy distinctions between television and real life. Thanks to our favorite fan magazines, *Photoplay* and *Modern Screen,* we understood that Allison's coma was induced, not by a tragic accident, but by Mia Farrow's own indecision about whether or not to leave the series and marry Frank Sinatra. Frank, Grandma emphasized, was old enough to be her father, her grandfather even, if we'd been living in some backward country. This Hollywood tryst became Grandmas's lifelong grievance. After *Peyton Place* was cancelled, after the couple's divorce, she would interrupt a new generation of TV characters to remind me how an "unnatural romance" had ruined one of the finest shows on television—"and all for nothing!"

But Grandma had more significant breaches of nature on her mind than May-December romances. My mother's untimely death was the backstory that informed most of our conversations. Even idle remarks about the weather inevitably reminded us that my mother, age twenty-seven, had died on an unseasonably cold November day giving birth to my brother, Mark. That was our family's ongoing cliff-hanger, because Grandma, who'd survived the Great Depression and who was struggling through a personal one, refused to equivocate with me. My mother was irreplaceable, and I would have to ration my expectations.

My early need for embellishment scared Grandma and also put her at odds with my father, an only child who'd always been comforted by what his parents referred to as *play pretties*, the southern term for toys they hoped would "take his mind off things." A lawyer born into a family of lawyers, he'd refused to exercise his legal options and investigate the suspicious circumstances surrounding Mother's fatal C-section—"so we can move on with our lives." And he'd been even more adamant about not wanting to arbitrate the loss with me. His opinion, which became a family edict, was that at two I couldn't process death and should be told—simply—that Jean Crane Miller had left for parts unknown and would not be returning to us.

Subsequently my father, Wesley, found consolation in a succession of *play pretties* who called him "Wes" and led him through multiple marriages. A short, charming man, diminished as much by circumstance as stature, he became known as the "Tahlequah Mickey Rooney" and was just as gregarious. In between marriages, he coped with grief—and two small children—by keeping us on a fixed social agenda, at least in the evenings. We spent Wednesday nights and weekends with Grandma and Grandpa Crane, Tuesday and Sunday nights with his parents, Monday nights with the soda jerk at the local Rexall store, and Thursday nights with the family of our state representative, who'd been elected to more responsibility than he'd anticipated.

We also grew up with an assortment of housekeepers who were responsible for the day watch, and one of them— we'll call her *Sally*—first introduced me to afternoon soap operas. In between episodes, which often brought us both to tears, Sally would indulge in prolonged bubble baths, barricading herself in the bathroom. If we disturbed her by requesting, say, Kool-Aid refills, she'd bellow, "I'll box your jaws" with the same Broderick Crawford–like authority we witnessed on *Highway Patrol.*

Highway Patrol and *Dragnet,* televised in black and white, had already made such a profound impression on me that, even before I was old enough for school, I started fixating on "distinguishing characteristics" in case any of us— besides Mother—ever went missing. I always looked for the colors in us, and I still recall our family in that way—my father's red ties, accenting his dark Cherokee undertones; Grandma Crane's navy sweaters, steadying her anxious blue eyes; and Grandma Miller's dangling silver "ear bobs," offsetting her deceptively soft cheeks, rouged to fullness. I also had a description ready for Sally, if we ever needed to report her. Even though she wore a pink, heart-shaped locket, her face was a clenched brown fist, exploding through layers of bubbles.

Fortunately Sally never followed through with her threats against us, partly because we'd slip into the spare bedroom to call Grandma Miller. A diminutive woman of Scottish-Cherokee descent—she was just under five feet—Grandma Miller would always phone right back, while we listened in on the extension, and tell Sally, "If you persist in yelling at the children, I'm going to have to shoot you."

Grandma Miller had her own kind of pioneer eloquence, but throughout these exchanges, I longed for my mother's voice in the conversational lapses, fantasizing that she might have suggested macaroni and cheese for dinner or reminded us to put on clean socks for the church picnic. I watched for her most often on Monday afternoons, when I'd grow anxious about the impending darkness and wonder who'd be sitting beside me later at the Rexall counter.

Since Mother was so vague to me, even the drugstore shadows had begun to look familiar, and I was routinely startled when they darted past us.

Though my father had mother-proofed our house, so that no pictures of her remained, my grandparents Crane displayed numerous photos of her—her long dark hair swept back Hollywood style, suggesting to me at first that I was the daughter of a generation of women, those dated fashion models who were so recognizable in Grandma's Montgomery Ward catalogs and *Good Housekeeping* magazines. It wasn't until later that I became convinced I was the child of actress Jeanne Crain, whom I'd seen so often on the late show.

I was too young to read and catch spelling distinctions—*Crain* with an *i*. I heard the name in my heart—in a household that never enforced bedtime and that answered painful questions by turning up the volume on the television. I'd caught similar programs more than once with Sally: glamorous young woman abandons family for a life of fame and fortune, only to regret her decision later and return to her loved ones with open arms.

Except that my mother was dead—as in *forever*. When I was six, cutting out a construction paper Valentine for my on-screen mother, Grandma Crane took me for a long drive and told me the truth that was to become the bond between us.

Grandma and I were almost always on the road after that, and her car—she never drove any make but Buick—became our unlikely sanctuary, where we'd both been indiscreet while admiring the hills in the distance. Grandma had admitted she could no longer cry, and I had *storied. Storying* was Grandma's word for my tendency—not to lie—but to narrate myself through the gaps in life. "You don't want to keep *storying* to yourself, Sister," she told me, her eyes locking with mine in the rearview mirror and sparing me as much directness as possible. "This Jeanne Crain you keep seeing on television is no relation of ours."

❧

The year before my mother died, Jeanne Crain starred in the movie Dangerous Crossings, *all about a young wife having a mental breakdown on the high seas. In real life, Jeanne Crain was to have seven children and receive many other blessings, including length of days.*

❧

Thanks to a booster cushion, Grandma sat tall behind the wheel and was not without her own mystique. The only one of our family members to hail from the East—she was born in Indiana—Grandma, aka Gayle Mills Crane, was generally considered our most exotic relative, though she'd moved to Oklahoma when she was seven and had no clear memory of that monumental journey.

For the most part, she'd devoted her life to short trips and kept a stash of Oklahoma/Arkansas/Missouri roadmaps bundled together in her glove compartment. Sometimes, though, she did reminisce about driving to Washington state with her daughter-in-law to take a car to my soldier uncle during World War II. The owner of the local Texaco had plotted out an itinerary for her, and she'd saved the travelogue as a reminder of where she had been and of the woman who'd befriended her in the Seattle train depot. She'd fallen ill, and the young mother had brought her a Coke, refusing to take any money in exchange. This single act of kindness had become more significant to Grandma than any tourist attraction. One of her lifelong regrets— and she had many—was that she'd failed to ask this bene- factor for her name.

Names took on added importance for Grandma, because Gayle was, in reality, her middle name, and she didn't trust any of us enough to reveal the first name she had dismissed as "embarrassing." She even allowed as how she'd altered the spelling of *Gail* during her teenage years out of regard for a teacher named *Gayle* who'd boarded with the family. But that was as far as she would go with any of us—even me—because she was always committed to holding herself in check. She eventually had a buzzer installed in one of her Buicks that went off every time she exceeded the speed limit, which meant we were constantly bracing ourselves for the unexpected jolt of her brakes—and of life.

One of our favorite outings was the ninety-mile trip we regularly made to Eads Brothers Furniture warehouse in Ft. Smith, Arkansas, to select items for my grandfather's store. As soon as I started school, Grandma taught me how to decipher the discount prices coded into the merchandise tags, alerting me to our privileged status. We were in on the deception, and somehow that caused her to abandon—at least when it came to furniture—any pretenses of her own. A frugal woman by nature, she bought whatever items she liked for her house, whether they matched her décor or not.

As a result, Grandma's living room was what I look back on as "post-depression existentialism." French provincial tables were paired with early American sofas—floral print—and velvet paintings. All against a backdrop of family photographs that reconciled the incongruities. The last photo of my mother showed her in the same room, color-coordinated then with easier contours and custom pillows. "We didn't have as many pictures and other fancy things," Grandma would say, "but somehow we managed to become our own decorations."

Sometimes she sounded almost biblical, which I suspect hearkened back to her school days, when she'd been required to memorize long passages of the Bible, "Thanatopsis," and "Ode to Solitude." A former science teacher, raised a Baptist and hardwired for the classics, she dabbled in *storying* herself by using family members to make her moral points on a grand scale. When I joined her before one of our trips by thanking God for our blessings, she likened me to my angel of a mother, a mathematical genius and first-chair clarinet player, who was looking down on us from Heaven. If she caught me sticking a wad of Doublemint gum under her dashboard, she'd say I was reminding her more and more of Grandma Miller.

Her issues with Grandma Miller, Leah, were more philosophical than personal. Grandma Miller had a reputation for, among other things, being a traffic violator. She had sideswiped a pickup in the Safeway parking lot but had left the scene of the accident because, as she explained to the officer who followed her home, she had ice cream she needed to get in the freezer and had intended to settle up later. Another time she had rammed into a young couple's station wagon, but had threatened to sue them instead, rationalizing that everyone in Tahlequah knew she was a bad driver and had a responsibility to keep out of her way. In other words, she did everything she could to perpetuate her image as a *public menace.*

Though I think Grandma Crane, who'd never crossed a yellow line in her life, had a grudging respect for this kind of defiance, she was always careful to emphasize the importance of "family examples"—good and bad. In her own way she'd elevated our relatives, "connections," to pantheon status, and we spent much of our road time regaling each other with our own *Odyssey* of family stories, told more than once and bound together with familiar refrains that helped us count off the miles—and the years.

ɔ

Infant Redbird was the descendant of those Cherokees who were forced to make the grueling trek to Oklahoma over what was to eventually become known as the Trail of Tears. "Infant" was his given name, bestowed upon him by English-speaking midwives who couldn't

*interpret his mother's endearments and filled out his
birth certificate generically. Mr. Redbird was well into
his eighties when he finally departed this life, but he
was still eulogized as "Infant" and his passing felt
premature.*

~

Though I wasn't without grandfathers, and dutiful ones
at that, they figured into our stories only occasionally. For
despite the fact that my grandmothers, as females, hadn't
even been allowed to serve on juries in Oklahoma until the
1950s, they were the de facto heads of their families. Both
women had worked outside the home—as teachers—and
both always drove their own cars, literally going their separate ways. Many years later Grandma Miller even opposed
the Equal Rights Amendment on the grounds that she'd
always considered herself superior and felt that equality
would be a step backward for her.

One story Grandma Crane and I *did* remember from
time to time was that Grandpa Oliver Crane, a medic in
World War I, had found his cousin Opal's photograph
in the wallet of a fallen soldier he'd been attending on a
French battlefield. He'd been on such a long tour of duty
he hadn't even heard that Opal had married during his
absence.

Then sometimes, when we'd stop at a roadside Dairy
Queen to indulge ourselves, we'd speak bemusedly about
how Grandpa had once made a verbal agreement to sell one
of his furniture stores, later received a much higher offer,
but kept his word and honored his original commitment.
"Go figure," Grandma would say, but it was hard to get a
read on how she really felt about Grandpa or her marriage.
They were an honorable couple who had lost much more
than a child between them.

Grandpa Miller, Will, was similarly shortchanged in
family lore, except for a few tales of his courtroom antics.

Known as a spirited defense attorney, he had once done such an admirable job of exonerating a murder defendant that a Tahlequah jury had returned to find one of the witnesses guilty.

Later Grandpa Miller had almost become subject to prosecution himself, when he and some cronies had bought a treasure map, headed out with pickaxes to Ft. Smith, Arkansas, to dig for buried gold, and inadvertently struck a water main before eluding authorities.

For the most part, though, our favorite stories tended to center around the family trickster and true-life felon, Grandma Miller's ne'er-do-well brother, Alton Parker Boyd, a printer by trade, who had a penchant for stealing typewriters, forging checks, and sweet-talking women of means. Grandma Miller was his primary victim. All Alton had to do was tell her that despite her detractors, including the Methodist minister, she was the finest pianist he'd ever heard. Grandma didn't even have to sign the checks for him; his forgery skills took care of that. She simply did her part by not pressing charges.

According to my father—and Grandma Crane and I would always pull off the highway and dig into our road snacks to savor this story—Alton had actually been imprisoned once in Utah for burglary. Outraged, Grandma Miller and her sister had immediately driven to Salt Lake City and demanded a meeting with the state's governor, who broke under pressure and finally agreed to pardon Alton on the condition that none of the family ever return to Utah again.

Besides providing us with stories from the Miller side of the family, my father also insinuated himself into my road kinship with Grandma in a different way, by setting up competing trips, so we could "cross borders together" and rehabilitate Oklahoma's image outside the state. For reasons I never fully understood, he seemed overly worried that *y'all* and other Oklahoma expressions that slipped so fluently from our tongues might subject us, even limit us, to the dust bowl stereotypes that still lingered from *The Grapes of Wrath,* the one book he wouldn't allow us to read.

Ironically, he was as adamant about banning *The Grapes of Wrath* as Grandma was about tuning out *The Waltons.* Not that he was the least bit offended by the book's so-called profanity. Cursing didn't bother him; he loved to curse himself. And not that he didn't admire Steinbeck's characters—the Joads had fortitude. He just didn't want us squeezed into the jalopy with them or with Jethro Clampett.

So, unlike Grandma, he drove defensively—in a social context. No blue jeans or chewing gum for us, not when his foot was on the gas pedal. To his way of thinking, our Oklahoma license plate obligated us to ambassador-like decorum. Before we headed down Route 66, we spit-polished the sedan and put on our Sunday finest. We were without fail the best-dressed, most well-mannered family to visit any Stuckey's of the 1960s. On at least two occasions, other tourists—in ball caps and Bermuda shorts—mistakenly identified us as traveling missionaries. My father *did* bring a zealot's fervor to these outings. In between stops, he would have us read aloud from the *Oklahoma Almanac,* and he regularly drilled us on *get*—not *git.*

Once, after a particularly ponderous stretch of highway, we arrived at Meramec Caverns in Missouri, where a guide commandeered us and some Japanese sightseers into the deepest recesses of the cave without letting anyone get a word in edgewise. She had an agenda and announced we were about to experience a rare moment of absolute darkness and SILENCE. With that, she switched off the lights, and my seven-year-old brother, his dress shoes squeaking in the void, decided to go global, rising to full volume to declare, "Oklahoma City was the first place in America to *get* parking meters—y'all." Later he had his photo taken by one of the Japanese women, and he gave it and a pecan log to Grandma as souvenirs.

Mark wasn't as accustomed to traveling with Grandma as I was and didn't know how empty a car could be without her. He delivered furniture with Grandpa and also formed an exclusive "guys only" relationship with Wesley. For as much as Wesley loved and feared women—his mother—he valued the patriarchy even more. When doctors told him that Mark and I both needed our tonsils removed, Wesley, whose friend had just lost a child during a tonsillectomy, agreed to let me undergo the surgery but couldn't, he admitted, take the risk with Mark. Grandma Crane consoled me by slipping me soothing chunks of ice while I was in recovery and pointing out my advantage—I'd be healthier. But she didn't indulge me beyond that; tradeoffs were her specialty.

∿

Grandma and Grandpa Miller had over fifty nieces and nephews. Consequently, when they set out on road trips to the World's Fair and other spectacles, they never considered patronizing what they called "motor lodges." They stayed with family, except for once, when they found themselves off course and knocked on the door of presumed strangers, who graciously offered them shelter for the night. It wasn't until the next morning that the man of the house reminded Grandpa that, during a stint as county attorney, Grandpa had sent him to prison for cattle theft. The man—guilty, he admitted—bore no grudges and invited Grandma and Grandpa to visit often.

∿

In many ways, even my relationship with Grandma Crane was a trade-off—for both of us. I'd become her second-generation daughter, and she'd become my older-than-usual mother. The age difference alone was enough to confound us, particularly when our neighbors would call it to our attention. One well-meaning young mother had once offered to help Grandma find new clothes for me that weren't so out-of-date, embarrassing Grandma to such an extent that she started giving me free rein in department stores and letting me put together my own ill-matched wardrobe.

She also felt compelled to be as "fun" as my friends' mothers and pressured herself into hosting a sixth-grade slumber party for me. It went beautifully—the girls said they'd never had such a good time—until we were just getting ready for bed, and Grandma asked if anyone was constipated.

I struggled to live up to my role, too, by adding to the collection of odds and ends my mother had given Grandma over the years—the miniature radio, the Eversharp pencil set, and the kitchen clock that had started to hum. Supposedly *Mother*—the name was awkward for me—had already bought and wrapped Christmas gifts before her death, and Wesley had distributed them to everyone. Since Grandma had always been partial to the clock, I suspected it had been her present that fateful holiday. But she lovingly displayed all the keepsakes throughout the house.

My contributions seemed to touch her as well, though she never relied on them. I remember the time I gave her what I thought would be the perfect gift, a poodle pin cushion, so unique that if you pulled its tail it became a measuring tape, but it was too fanciful for her tastes, and she left it on the dresser, next to the unopened bottle of *Intimate* perfume I'd gotten for her birthday.

Surprisingly, Grandpa seemed to empathize in his own quiet way by regularly wearing the plaid work shirts I always bought him during the holidays. I didn't know him well enough to reach beyond his gold-rimmed glasses and natural ruddiness to come up with more creative presents.

He spent most of his time at the furniture store and didn't interact with the family much, except for our formal conversations at dinner, when he'd talk about the day's proceeds and then offer to share them with Grandma as we planned our next excursion. "I want you girls to have a good time in Ft. Smith," he'd say, but occasionally he let me know that he expected our relationship to be more than just a routine transaction. One day he gave me the foreign coins he'd collected during his tour of duty in France, noting that the tarnished tokens weren't of any real value, except as a remembrance of his service and the principles that had taken him so far from home.

He'd brought back one more souvenir that was his alone—a gaping wound in his left leg, the result of flying shrapnel. Though he was entitled to disability compensation, he always refused it and did everything he could to disguise his injury. Sometimes I'd peek into his bedroom and spot him changing his bandage, but he'd politely wave me on, acknowledging the distance between us.

Even Grandma and I were finding it increasingly difficult to bridge this double-generation gap, and our frustrations began carrying over to our motor trips, especially as I began to make some calculations. "Do you realize," I ventured, on the verge of getting my driver's license and plotting out trips of my own, "that if someone added up all the miles we've driven roundtrip just to Muskogee, we've gone far enough to get to New York, to Los Angeles even, and we haven't really *been* anywhere?"

"Don't forget Decatur," she retorted, reminding me of our recent visit to one of her Arkansas homesteads, where she'd once made the mistake of raising chickens on the second floor to earn extra money. I could just hear her reciting "To a Waterfowl" above the cackle.

"Yeah, we'll always have Decatur," I said, suddenly turning on the radio.

We'd been through these tense exchanges before, like the time we'd had our "frank" conversation about sex and she'd forgotten herself, using Mother's relationship with Wesley to make her point about the dangers of infatuation. When I'd reminded her that I was the result of their "infatuation," she'd decided to forgo logic and explain, "Your mother could have had you with someone else."

We'd had yet another awkward conversation after some junior high friends and I had over-imbibed on cherry vodka and she'd distinguished me as the only girl, woman, she'd ever seen inebriated. She'd draped her arm around me, though, and eventually offered me a box of chocolate-covered cherries as an appealing alternative.

So this newest restlessness didn't take her by surprise—her speed buzzer was on, and, after all, she'd been hearing me replay Streisand's song lyrics "Gotta move, Gotta get out / Gotta leave this place," in between episodes of *Peyton Place* for the past several weeks. Somehow—and who could explain such a thing?—my aspirations were getting unwieldy inside the Buick, and I'd already announced my plans to leave for New York as soon as I was old enough to pursue an acting career.

To her credit, she didn't suggest that my dream might be unattainable—or that I might be trying to become the Jeanne Crain I'd misappropriated as a child. Instead, she asked if I'd like to drive for a while—we were en route to Tulsa to buy a La-Z-Boy recliner to go with her Louis IV end table. She'd pulled over to the side of the road, and I traded places with her, trying discretely to drop her booster cushion into the backseat. But the role reversal startled both of us, and she told me to keep my eyes on the road while she enjoyed the *sights* I referred to as *pastures*.

We both knew she was secretly hoping that, by the time I graduated from high school, I'd change my mind and learn to embrace my heritage. Even my father, who had cringed at being typecast as an Oklahoman himself, suddenly became Tahlequah's most ardent booster.

That summer our California relatives came to visit, and their trip happened to coincide with Tahlequah's rodeo parade. They insisted that they were not *rodeo people* but joined us on the street corner to watch the steady processional of cowboys/cowgirls, Cherokee honor guards, baton twirlers, Shriners, football stars, and even our dog Tuffy. At one point my cousin turned to my father and asked, "Why are all these different people—and animals—marching through Tahlequah?" He hesitated a moment, shifting his focus from the gold horse atop the dry goods store to the gazebo on the town square. Then he replied, matter-of-factly, that we were "the Athens of northeast Oklahoma," which was for my ears as much as hers.

That's how my father kept bewildering us. He'd served in Hawaii during World War II and traveled frequently to cities like Chicago via his work on the National Mediation Board, yet he still envisioned Tahlequah as some sort of hub, particularly after Grandpa Miller began suffering from dementia and telling us about Perry Mason's visits to the local nursing home. Though Wesley, who'd always admired his father's intellect, couldn't bear the hurt of spending time with Grandpa during his decline, he suddenly overcompensated by becoming almost as fanciful himself.

When rumors abounded that James Earl Ray, the assassin of Martin Luther King, had been spotted in Tahlequah, Wesley went searching for him. When another story circulated that psychic Jeanne Dixon had predicted that an axe murderer would go on a rampage through town, he double-bolted his doors. And years later when word spread that kidnapped newspaper heiress, Patricia Hearst, was buying supplies at the new Wal-Mart, he rushed to the store with a shopping list and camera.

His born-again provincialism even impacted him

professionally. When a mentally disturbed man came to Tahlequah proclaiming himself to be one of the Three Stooges, Wesley used "Curly" as a celebrity character witness for a woman trying to regain credibility in a custody battle. We were all mystified. Apparently Wesley had begun swapping urban legends for rural ones, a mythic compromise that, along with Grandpa's lingering confusion, lowered expectations for everyone.

Ultimately it had been Grandpa Miller's decline that had put Mark and me on a first-name basis with Wesley. Grandpa was considerably older than our other grandparents, and we'd never really known him well enough to develop personal relationships with him. Even so, we both felt obliged to take Wesley's place at the deathbed vigils Grandma regularly hosted in Grandpa's honor. As one of our cousins put it, Wesley and Grandpa were the only relatives who never showed up for these grim but fully catered occasions. And so over time, after months of eating cocktail sandwiches and listening for the "death rattle," Mark and I came to regard our father as a kind of backsliding older sibling.

If Wesley was the least bit remorseful about expecting his teenaged children to take on these adult responsibilities, he gave no such indication, even after Grandpa died—or as Wesley euphemized the loss, "graduated to glory." Instead, he continued to comfort himself with the smallness he'd been embracing since Grandpa's diagnosis. He loved to tell the story about the three Cherokee elders who'd promised to meet after the Trail of Tears to decide on the permanent location for their new capital. When one of the three didn't appear as expected—and this became our personal allegory—the other two took the initiative and called their new home, *Tahlequah,* "Two are enough."

But Tahlequah, population seven thousand or so in the late 1960s, wasn't enough for me, at least then. That's when

I started trying to mainstream my frustrations by writing stories entitled "Godzilla vs. Tahlequah," "Gidget Goes to Tahlequah," and "On the Road to Tahlequah," all of them serials promising even more local mayhem in upcoming installments.

∾

My grandmother's younger sisters, Leona and Geral-
dine, survived an arduous trip from Indiana to Okla-
homa and the 1918 flu pandemic but died within three
weeks of each other while still in their late teens, one
girl from meningitis, the other from peritonitis. I have
inherited Geraldine's aging copy of A Tale of Two Cities, *which is delicately inscribed with her name, making*
the story hers forever.

∾

I had always loved books and more and more they became my means of transit out of Oklahoma, taking me the places Grandma couldn't. Early on I'd been a fan of the Nancy Drew stories. After all, I was a motherless daughter with a lawyer father, grumpy housekeeper, and mysterious neighbors. But I'd lost interest in the novels after discovering that Carolyn Keene was a publishing-house pseudonym. In fact, my first fully realized work, written while I was in junior high, was entitled *The End of Nancy Drew*, which resolved the serial's personal cliffhangers by marrying off all the lead characters to each other.

It was the truth—and subterfuge—behind *Carolyn Keene* that eventually became my reality check with fiction. There had been lots of Carolyn Keenes, just as there'd been lots of Lassies, and I learned that I was story-beholden to those authors who owned their names. Seeing their pictures on book jackets and reading their mini-biographies made my fictional departures all the more credible for me.

The first serious novel that made a profound impression on me was Betty Smith's *A Tree Grows in Brooklyn*, which I discovered during puberty. Not only did I relate to Betty's adolescent heroine, I also recognized the common flora, "the only tree that grows out of cement," that Betty described so artfully in the companion poem that introduces the book. I even became intrigued with the author herself and bought my next *Betty Smith* title without bothering to read the jacket copy.

Needless to say, *Joy in the Morning,* the mildly explicit story of a young married couple, was a tantalizing read for a teenager—and a risky one. My math teacher caught me secreting the paperback inside the folds of *Adventures in Algebra* and sent me to the principal's office for dog-earing page 37. Clearly Betty and I'd gone the distance with each other.

Still another book, *The Hunt for the Tsar,* by New York reporter Guy Richards, transported me to Bolshevik Russia and took my reading experience to a whole new level— author contact. Though purportedly nonfiction, the book made the fanciful claim that the Romanovs had escaped assassination and were living in luxurious safe havens around the world. This was an inviting premise for someone like me, who'd once mistaken Jeanne Crain for her long-lost mother. I immediately wrote a fan letter to Guy, noting that I would be coming to New York to attend the American Academy of Dramatic Arts during the summer and hoped to meet him for coffee while I was "in the city." He graciously replied and included his phone number—along with a notice about an upcoming reunion of all the Romanov claimants. It was an exciting time.

"Don't trick yourself, Sister," Grandma told me, but I'd already filled out the paperwork for the American Academy, spent my birthday money on a subscription to *Variety,* and set aside part of my college tuition to cover my residency at the Martha Washington Hotel for Women. The hotel, by the way, came highly recommended—it's where Anne Welles had stayed in *Valley of the Dolls.*

In retrospect, what makes my escape story almost as whimsical as the Romanov tale is that my family, despite its reservations, never prohibited me from going to New York—as long as I promised to come back to college in Tahlequah that fall. My father did have an attorney friend who lived in the city, and he volunteered to check in on me from time to time. And our banker's brother-in-law, also a New Yorker and a struggling actor, had promised to touch base with me, too—after his letter warning me not to make the trip had failed to dissuade me. But that was as far as the family itself could extend the protective boundaries of Tahlequah.

I should emphasize that I don't think Grandma Crane and Wesley were naïve or careless where I was concerned. In fact they were worldlier than many of their fashionably cautious friends. They'd already lost Mother in familiar territory and had long since acknowledged that there were no real safeguards in life.

∽

After my mother's death, the family received hundreds of condolence cards, which Grandma Crane saved for me in my very own cedar chest. One note was on the letterhead of Hollywood gossip columnist Hedda Hopper, but it was from her secretary at the time, a former Tahlequah girl, who still felt close to us in grief.

∼

By the time I left for New York, the biggest star on anyone's map, I'd become a student as well as a fan of *Peyton Place*. I'd even listed acting experience with Dorothy Malone on my résumé, rationalizing that Dorothy and I *had* actually spent a lot of Thursday evenings together. Ours just wasn't a reciprocal relationship.

My application to the Academy must have been convincing, because I was almost immediately accepted on the condition that I do a final audition. I was still rehearsing when I landed at La Guardia and went straight to the Academy so as not to delay my stardom a moment longer. My performance piece was Blanche's monologue from *A Street-car Named Desire*—the narration in which she chronicles the loss of not just her family, but also Belle Reeve, their plantation, proclaiming to her brother-in-law, Stanley, "I, I, I took the blows in my face and my body!"

One very complimentary evaluator noted that I must be a method actress, for I was still in character—southern drawl intact—a full hour after my performance. Somehow, it hadn't dawned on these theater professionals that, as a fourth-generation Oklahoman, I had a genuine claim to the drawl, even to a pronounced twang.

I had a short run at the Academy. The director herself called me to her office a few days later and delivered her own somber assessment on behalf of the entire faculty: "You simply can't continue to perform Shakespeare, even in practice, saying *woooman*. It's so un-Elizabethan and so not New York. Have you ever considered any other profession?" I told her that I'd given some thought to becoming a writer, to which she quickly responded, "Then that's what you must do—immediately!" So at her suggestion I returned Tahlequah to pursue my calling as a writer, but not before gracing her with the defining performance of my not-so-brilliant career. Smiling through the disappointment, I somehow managed to exit gracefully, stage right, through the rubble of my first broken dream.

I left New York with one other regret apart from my deferred stardom. I didn't have time to follow through with Guy Richards—or to get friendly with the Romanovs. That's why in retrospect my family regards this trip as a *Law and Order* episode that just never came to fruition.

∾

The legendary inaugural first lady of our country,
Martha Washington, who drank only for medicinal
purposes and mended flags with Betsy Ross in her front
parlor, is not to be confused with her alter ego, whose
persona informed the hotel where I stayed in New York.
That Martha Washington, also a foremother—and the
patron saint of wayward travelers—could write her
own tantalizing memoir, which would be banned in
Tahlequah.

~

When I got back home, safe, but just as determined to
leave again, Grandma drove me to the outskirts of town
and directed my attention to a new Chamber of Com-
merce billboard that read: "Are you sure you couldn't find
it in Tahlequah?" A graduating senior had spray-painted
a big red *X* over *it in,* asking the more profound question:
"Are you sure you couldn't find Tahlequah?" I didn't have
a good answer for Grandma—or myself—except that, like
Wesley, I was beginning to chafe at the stereotypical, *Grapes
of Wrath* image many had of our state. The very fact I'd
been expelled from acting school because of my accent only
accentuated those feelings, and I started taking issue with
Grandma herself whenever she said, "I reckon," which, I believed, was too Oklahoma sounding to serve any of us well.

She also had some tough words for me when I announced that, because of my "artistic differences" with the
Academy, I feared I might be on the verge of a nervous
breakdown. I'd heard Grandma Miller use this same declaration with great effect over the years, but Grandma Crane,
who'd just advanced me a loan, wasn't impressed. "Honey,"
she said, flipping on her headlights even though it was only
late afternoon, "you just can't afford a nervous breakdown.
If you really have your heart set on one, you'll need to put
yourself on a budget, save up, and then let go."

So advised, I finally found a job at the *Cherokee County*

Chronicle, where my professional writing career *almost* got off to a promising start. My assignment was to write a weekly column for the paper that listed all of the traffic violations, assault charges, and divorce petitions filed in our county. "About Tahlequah"—generic and personal at the same time—soon became one of the most popular columns in the *Chronicle*, and I started regaining my confidence.

One week I even filled in as layout artist, putting together what I thought was an especially eye-catching edition, but the phone calls started coming in the minute the paper hit Main Street. I'd inadvertently placed an arthritis ad next to the obituaries that read, "Don't wake up with that stiff feeling," resulting in my immediate dismissal. So "About Tahlequah" became the platform for another local writer, also the staff astrologer, who was always on the lookout for tricky alignments.

∽

Once when I attended a friend's citizenship ceremony in Tulsa, I found myself in a crowded auditorium sitting next to a former step-uncle, who introduced himself after seeing my name badge. His wife was from Scandinavia, I think; my friend from Germany; and the missing stepmother from parts unknown. Years before, Grandma Miller had phoned the stepmother to establish some new boundaries, explaining that Tahlequah simply didn't exist for women who abused her grandchildren. That was Grandma's specialty—the fine art of cartography. It's amazing how quickly you can take a place off somebody's map if you have a brother named Alton and know how to stake your own territory.

∽

Phones didn't ring late in 1970s Tahlequah—either capriciously or randomly. Grandma and I both knew before she answered that midnight call November 16 that Grandpa, who'd been recovering from thyroid surgery in the Muskogee hospital, was dead. At the time, I was living next door in her "rent house" while I worked on my novel, but we'd decided to spend the evening together so we could catch up on our television shows.

It was clear what we had to do, because we'd done it so many times before—drive to Muskogee. But I would have to be the one behind the wheel—and not just as an indulgence. She would need to rely on me.

For once we didn't have a lot of road stories to share—they'd been eclipsed by circumstance. Grandpa had passed away on the nineteenth anniversary of my mother's death, and Grandma, who'd dreamed of becoming a doctor and who'd settled instead for being an educator, was stunned by the coincidence. Grief, she speculated, resorting to clichés, had come full circle, and neither of us could make sense—much less science—out of the peculiar and heartbreaking orbit.

As soon as we arrived at the hospital, we learned that Grandpa had died of *complications.* An understatement—he had aspirated in his sleep. Grandma winced at that news, reprimanded herself for coming home earlier in the day, and then asked to see him alone. She had things to say to him, she told the attending physician and me, but she wasn't gone long and gave no hint as to what transpired during those secret moments.

We didn't leave until close to dawn and had to strain to see our way through the morning darkness—literally and figuratively. Our Buick was one of the few cars on the road, and at one point we tried to comfort each other with what felt like an obligatory Uncle Alton tale. Once, while recovering in the Tahlequah hospital, he'd impersonated a local doctor and had himself transferred, via chartered ambulance, to a private room in Muskogee General. He'd also made sure to prescribe a generous dose of mood elevators for his "patient."

"Alton's going to outlive all of us," Grandma said, quick to respond, but I could hear the catch of irony in her voice as she considered how well Alton had fared in comparison to Grandpa.

Mostly, though, there was silence between us. Not just the silence of November 16, past and present, but the silence of all those intervening years, after the pronouncement of Mother's death had made everything else, including my stepmother's abuse, seem like small-talk between us. Now that Grandpa was dead and Mark was in trouble—drugs—even the squeak of my uneasy grip on the steering wheel was almost more than we could tolerate.

Grandma had told me once that return trips were always quicker, just a matter of reversing course, not navigating your way. But thirty miles stretched forever that night, and she admitted to me later that she didn't think we'd ever get home.

Even after we did arrive, she couldn't stop moving and suddenly started doing all of Grandpa's laundry, stretching his wet slacks on the aluminum frames she always used so she wouldn't have to iron. Then she was mopping, dusting, putting on a stew, all in anticipation of company. She paused only long enough to say that Grandpa had asked her earlier in the day to remind him of the date, and between her own deep breaths, she wondered aloud if he hadn't choked on what should have been said nineteen years earlier.

For not only had our family failed to confront Mother's doctor about what Mother herself had reported—excessive bleeding, complications, a quickly resanitized operating room—all of us, except for Grandpa Crane, had continued to go to him with *our* medical needs. Even after another young mother had died under similar circumstances. It was almost as if, by adhering to decorum, we were trying to sanction human recklessness, deeming it an act of God, aka thromboembolism, so we could memorialize Mother on a grander scale.

The pretense was catching up with us, though, and exposing our individual weaknesses. This same doctor had started making blatant sexual overtures toward me, and Wesley kept insisting we couldn't report him. His justification was that we lived in a small town—without many options—and didn't have any other physicians who were so clearly beholden to us. In other words, Wesley, like Mark, had come to rely on drugs, but he was addicted to prescription sedatives and couldn't risk alienating his supplier.

Later that morning, after we'd contacted most of the immediate family, Grandma finally asked me to get Mark on the phone, but I couldn't reach him. He was on a debate scholarship at Loyola University in California and had slipped so far away that even Grandma Miller couldn't get within shouting distance. Of course we'd tried family interventions—to no avail. We were living out our own version of *Leviticus* in reverse. Mother's death *begat* its own loss.

∽

My cousins' grandmother, Mrs. Stolper, came to the United States from France and regularly traveled from Muskogee to Tahlequah to pick up her grandchildren for visits. But she was so short, her feet couldn't reach the dimmer switch in her car. She was still determined to travel at night, though, and adapted by keeping her headlamps on high beam and wearing sunglasses to shield herself from the angry flashes of oncoming drivers. Some of us continue to watch for her, a phantom beacon, on lonely highways.

∽

Mark did not return to Tahlequah in time for Grandpa's funeral, choosing instead to attend a debate tournament. But he wasn't as indifferent as he seemed. Debate was more than a diversion for him; it was his balancing act, a way for him to use his gift with words to reconcile the opposing forces that were his legacy. When he finally did come home, steadying himself with a briefcase in each hand, I better understood the struggles of his life. Mark had to walk a fine line to distinguish himself from the grief that was his birthday.

By the time of Grandpa's death, I'd become ensconced in the English program at our local university, where writing and literature courses were *my* consolation and inspiration. I was particularly drawn to a specialty group of southern writers—those still writing from their hometowns—and tried to establish contact with them as I worked on my first novel. I knew that Harper Lee, author of the classic *To Kill a Mockingbird*, lived in Monroeville, Alabama, and I called Monroeville information, asking for her phone number. The operator replied, "Honey, Harper's number's unlisted, but she lives with her sister Alice, and I'll give you Alice's number." Sure enough, it worked, and I had a delightful conversation with Harper, which I forgot almost instantly, because I was so heartened to realize that one of America's greatest authors was only a book and a phone call away.

The highlight of my author-seeking years was visiting Eudora Welty at her home in Jackson, Mississippi. I thought her story "A Worn Path" was one of the most stunning character portraits I'd ever read, and I convinced a friend that we should drop by to see the famous writer en route to a meeting in New Orleans. I'd gotten Ms. Welty's address from *Contemporary Authors* and was too naïve to realize we might be intruding. To Ms. Welty's enormous credit, she was gracious and trusting enough to invite us inside.

My plan had been to chat with Ms. Welty about the subtleties of her own work and also to seek advice about my novel in progress, but she was preoccupied, not with metaphors, but heat. Her furnace was out, and we spent our time together, fledgling writer and Pulitzer winner, talking about how hard it was to find good repairmen. A few months later, she was scheduled to appear on Dick Cavett's television interview program, and I persuaded Grandma to stay up late so she could experience Ms. Welty's eloquence for herself. I can't recall Cavett's lead-in line but toward the end of the interview, Ms. Welty responded with the phrase, "Do you reckon?" My grandmother didn't say a word, but she cut her eyes toward me, smiled for the first time in months, and let me know that she had, indeed, been validated by a coincidence that was more to her liking.

The novel that I was working on was rejected by virtually every publisher in the country. As was my next novel. Both books had been set in exotic locales that I'd hoped to visit one day. It wasn't until I finally located a story in rural Oklahoma that I caught the attention of New York agents and got my first publishing contract. The irony didn't escape me, but I was quick to explain that my focus on Brady, the fictional town in *Remnants of Glory*, was merely a matter of expedience. And yes, it did bear a striking resemblance to Tahlequah.

News that I'd finally sold my book wasn't greeted as enthusiastically within the family as I'd anticipated. Grandma had always been wary of my publishing dreams, because, conditioned by her days as a furniture buyer, she kept looking for price tags with secret bargains we could decode. To make matters even worse, she'd formed an unlikely alliance with Grandma Miller, who'd gone so far as to rendezvous with one of my college professors at the Wagon Wheel restaurant on the outskirts of town, where she'd prevailed upon the woman to use any influence she had with me to keep me from becoming a writer.

Not that either grandmother was trying to deny me my dream, but as survivors of the Depression, both had serious concerns about what they termed my *livelihood*. As far as they were concerned I'd already used up my career wild card on my acting venture. One grandmother—I'll never know which—had actually submitted my name to several occupational mailing lists, and I was regularly receiving flyers featuring smartly dressed young poster women—all smiles—personifying such captions as "Your Career in Real Estate," "Your Future in Optometry," and "Opportunities in Electrolysis."

So I'd already gone on the defensive and thought I'd assuaged them when I got a short story included in *The New Infinity Review*. I'd even been paid, one-fifty, I reported. "One-hundred fifty dollars," Grandma Crane replied. "That's pretty good." But when I explained that I actually meant a dollar fifty, she wasn't amused.

Even the fact that my novel was being represented by two New York literary agents was of little comfort to her, and she wanted to know more about their backgrounds. One, I told her, was from Indiana, her home state, so she let down her guard a little, but when I added that the other was from the Blue Ridge Mountains of Virginia, Walton Country, she bristled with renewed concern, positioning herself for the face-off she'd been postponing for more than ten years. "Make no mistake about it," she began soberly, gripping my shoulders. "The Waltons are a family of easy marks." Clearly, in her view, my *storying* had gotten way out of hand.

The name of my new publisher was Seaview, which I found very poetic, very coastal, but I still had a lot to learn about publishing hierarchy. I was actually into the final draft of the book before my agents explained that Seaview was an imprint and that I was working for Playboy Enterprises. *Playboy* had been banned in Tahlequah, and women in shrouds were stalking any local businesses that sold the magazine. My career, I feared, was going to be jeopardized by the same community-think that had sent me to the principal's office with *Joy in the Morning*. Thankfully, my

Playboy connection wasn't outed until years later. Still, only a person with a healthy need for money would have risked taking a bunny-embossed check to a Tahlequah bank during the 1980s. I had nightmares.

∾

Kate Fite Smullen lived just outside of Tahlequah in a log cabin her husband had built for her by hand and named Echota, *the Cherokee word for contentment. In her heyday, Kate had traveled throughout the nation on the Chautauqua circuit, playing the role of the Cherokee Butterfly in such grand company as Helen Keller and William Jennings Bryan. Kate's husband later died in a freak accident, and she transformed her home into a museum of sorts. Visitors could find her fluttering just inside the parlor—in front of a wooden bowl marked: "Donations for the care and upkeep of Echota."*

∾

Getting a book contract didn't mean the novel was finished. My very patient editor, Sherry, who'd worked with the likes of acclaimed short story author Alice Munro, had gently suggested that I needed to show more of the dust in Oklahoma—and she wasn't speaking metaphorically. So Grandma and I took several short day trips so she could point out—in contrast—the hills and streams I'd been bypassing for years. "The Town Branch is more than just a creek," she explained to me, as if she were describing the mighty Mississippi instead of the branch coursing its way through the heart of Tahlequah. "It teaches us that, if we take our time and watch out for sharp rocks, we can usually wade across to each other."

Though Grandma took her role as "guide" seriously—and expressed delight at having the book dedicated to her and my childhood friend, Lori—she was "somewhat" uncomfortable with my heroine, Kate, who at ninety was looking back on her missed opportunities from the confines of a nursing home. Grandma rightfully assumed that, because Kate was older, some readers, aka our neighbors, might conclude that Kate was based on Grandma herself. Not that Grandma had any major difference of opinion with Kate, but the character had set aside her high principles to have an affair with her brother-in-law. Grandma wasn't about to judge Kate—she was family. She just didn't want any local speculation pairing her off with her own brother-in-law, whom she'd always found particularly unattractive.

In truth, Kate wasn't a fictional manifestation of my grandmother, but of an era of women who consistently turned away from their own pursuits to respond to the needs of others. My male muse had actually been the poet Samuel Taylor Coleridge, who'd never been able to finish his poem "Kubla Khan" because, in the midst of his inspiration, he had been called out on business and had felt obliged to go. However, my publicists at Seaview were already cautioning me to keep this creative backstory to myself, since it didn't exactly make for tantalizing copy.

That said, though, Grandma's spirit and life experience certainly did inform the book, and as I visited with her about her era, I got to know her more intimately. On one occasion, as I was trying to get a feel for Kate's mother, Cora, I asked Grandma what she was afraid of as a young woman. "Mad dogs," she replied without thinking, which struck me as a very unromantic, but nevertheless, accurate response from a pioneering perspective. For what could be more threatening than nature gone rabid? I wrote what Grandma said into the story as an exchange between Kate and Cora, but if Grandma ever made the connection, she didn't acknowledge it.

I also included some just-for-fun personal associations in the novel, originally calling one of the story's aspiring villains Wesley and scrambling the names of my agents Ginger Barber and Mary Evans for the cameo characters

Abner B. Rigger and Neva Ramsey. Wesley, by the way, was successfully battling bladder cancer, and I'd been driving him back and forth to Tulsa for his radiation treatments. In his case, thirty trips equaled a cure, but they were so carefully measured, our time together felt prescribed and lowered our tolerance for each other. He took exception to my light-hearted allusion to him, and I had to go through the manuscript with Liquid Paper substituting *Hardin,* a family surname, for his. It was a sticky proposition.

And there were other telling overlaps between *Remnants* and real life, despite the disclaimer at the front of the book. I'd been engaged to a young man whose aunt suffered from Down's syndrome, and Kate had a mentally challenged daughter who played a pivotal role in the novel. Also, Kate's father Guerney had the same philosophical bent as my great-grandfather Mills and had a stallion by the same name, Rabitjoie. But the disclaimer was true to this extent: even at that age—I was in my mid-twenties—I knew that there wasn't a book big enough or a hand steady enough to really do justice to my family.

∽

> Grandma Miller, who claimed to be related to the Confederate spy Belle Boyd and who had inherited her ancestor's roving nature, hadn't always traveled exclusively with Grandpa or her sisters. She had once fallen in love with another man, an indiscretion that had taken her to California but hadn't been powerful enough to keep her in such a foreign state. She eventually reconciled with Grandpa on the front porch of her sister's house in Tahlequah, where they recommitted themselves to what they considered the World's Fair of ordinary existence.

∼

Mark had transferred back to our local university and, without Wesley's knowledge, arranged for our "family doctor" to finally remove his tonsils. Grandma and I didn't even know until the very last minute and rushed to the hospital, only to meet the doctor coming out of surgery. Feeling vindicated, he told us he'd been able to complete the operation in a matter of minutes and snapped his fingers to emphasize his agility and expertise.

At first Mark did seem fine, with only the usual post-op nausea and sore throat, but by evening he was losing large quantities of blood. I'd never seen Grandma so frantic. She tried to get in touch with the doctor, who sent back word through an aide that he wasn't the least bit alarmed and thought Grandma should go home—"for some rest." In the meantime, though, Mark's blood pressure had started dropping steadily, and Grandma, ashen herself, turned to one of the nurses and suddenly understood: "This is just how that man let my daughter die."

The nurse, who had been on duty the night of Mother's death, disappeared for a few minutes, then returned with the doctor, who became agitated himself after he examined Mark. The buzz in the hallway was that no one had ever seen him so discomfited, and we'd overheard the speculation, too. Though none of the staff would say so directly, he'd more than likely cut an artery in Mark's throat that morning, and to complicate the situation, the hospital was completely out of Mark's blood type. Within minutes, the Highway Patrol was being dispatched to an outlying hospital to transport four pints back to Tahlequah so Mark could receive multiple transfusions.

Mark was only semiconscious by then, and even as we paced the length of his hospital bed, my thoughts gradually turned to my mother and the difference she could have made in all our lives. I was still trying to piece together what little information I'd learned about her, relying on the sketchy, unemotional details that Grandma had been able to share with me over the years. A brilliant student, she had graduated from the local university at seventeen. She'd also made many devoted friends and had once bought a hat with a feather so big that it had embarrassed Wesley. Mostly, though, Mother was my own creation, the personification of everything that seemed to be missing for us.

Hours later, after we were assured Mark would make a full recovery, it became more and more apparent that Grandma would not. Any illusions that had helped her cope with Mother's death were gone, and she blamed herself as much as anyone else—she should have acknowledged her sense of foreboding, seen the signs sooner, and called in another doctor. We'd moved to the same waiting room where she'd taken charge of Mother's personal effects in 1954, and she pulled back a moment to stare at the outdated vending machine and green vinyl couch before making her final declaration: her daughter, Jean, had bled to death.

And in her mind, at least, she had no doubts. She didn't cry and was even civil, though reserved, when the doctor stopped in to tell us Mark was resting peacefully. Of course, I wanted her to say more, to hold this man directly accountable and make him squirm, repent maybe. But that wasn't her style, and there was remarkable candor in the way she overcame her weariness, rose to her full stature, and walked past him without saying another word. *Fiction* was the realm for bolder voices.

∿

My mother tried to get in touch with Grandma when she was on her Washington trip, because Grandma had not checked in with the family like she'd promised. Addressing the letter to her at Hostess House in Seattle, Mother implored, "The least you can do is write us a note. We didn't hear from you for five days after you left." Grandma kept the letter in an old lingerie box with her college diploma and marriage certificate, perhaps as a reminder, amongst these accomplishments,

*of the postcard she'd failed to send before Mother herself
had traveled beyond our reach.*

~

As *Remnants* moved closer to publication, I began receiving marketing questionnaires from Seaview's publicity
department, trying to target ways to promote the novel. At
one point I was asked to list all of the celebrities living in
Tahlequah who might endorse the book. I wrote back that
the only celebrity Tahlequah had ever produced was Mr. Ed,
the talking horse, but unfortunately he'd passed away.

Inadvertently I'd given Seaview publicists their angle—
Country Girl Writes Her Way to the Big Apple. I wasn't
thrilled with the concept, but at least I was going to New
York and appearing in a promotional film, which, I fantasized, might even revive my acting career and help me relocate to the city permanently.

Right before I left, Grandma and I drove State Highway
10 along the Illinois River, past Kate Smullen's house and
Eagle's Bluff, so she could resort to some fiction herself and
confide in me about her cousin Lucy—she hadn't wanted
to alarm me before—who'd gone to New York in the 1950s
and hadn't been heard from since.

Grandma was afraid for me, much more so than when I'd
headed out for the Academy as a teenager. That's what the
coincidental deaths of my mother and grandfather, not to
mention Mark's close call, had done to her. For as horrify-
ing as my mother's loss had been for Grandma, she'd found
default comfort in the notion that it had granted the rest of
her family some sort of asylum, that something so out of
sync with the natural order could never happen to us again.

A freak twister in *Remnants*, the only other major personal overlap with the book, makes that point for her, up-
ending the tiny community of Brady, even though Indian
myth had always promised that no tornado would ever

strike the town—it was nestled in a valley, protected by the hills.

She also wanted to talk about Vaud, the man I'd been engaged to, who'd called a few nights before to pick up some of his record albums. Though she would never admit it, she and Grandma Miller were both put off by his aunt's Down syndrome.

"So," she ventured, just as casually as if she'd been directing my attention to a mildly confusing road sign in the distance, "does it look like you two will be getting back together?"

"No," I told her. "He thinks we're too peculiar."

"Well, supposing for a minute Wesley is odd," she said. "That doesn't mean we all are." She was obviously miffed and relieved at the same time. "Just promise me—"

"I'll keep an eye out for Lucy," I told her and, to seal our deal, accepted the fold-up rain cap she'd gotten me that bore the image of the Statue of Liberty with the blurb *Liberty State Bank in Tahlequah—Your Hometown Advantage.* The gift was her way of helping me keep the trip in perspective, because, as excited as I was about going to New York again and appearing in the film, I was clearly out of sync with the city itself. When Ginger and Mary called, asking if I'd like to see the Yankees during my visit, I was so overcome by regionalism and athletic ignorance, I replied, "Yankees, won't we be seeing plenty of them as it is?"

I displayed the same lack of sophistication once I arrived and began spending time with Sherry. She had to pull me aside early on in our relationship to explain that I simply could not go up and down the streets of Manhattan saying "hi" to everyone—I was attracting attention. The key, she informed me, to surviving in New York was to pretend I didn't notice anyone or anything. A few blocks later we encountered a man dressed in a tomato costume, and one of the hardest things I've ever had do was feign my indifference.

Indoors, though, New York felt like home territory, especially as I began to discover myself as a writer. Mary and Ginger worked with me patiently, going over every line of the book and actually reading parts of the chapters aloud, so I could develop a sharper ear for the story. Many of my southern expressions weren't resonating with the copyeditors, and we had to decide which words to champion. We were stuck on *blinky*, the expression my family—and Ginger's—had always used to describe milk on the verge of becoming sour. Never mind my *accent*. As Ginger reminisced about her Virginia childhood, she reverted to *y'all* herself and finally declared, "*blinky*'s staying" with such conviction that I no longer worried about saying *wooooman* in Seaview's promotional film.

The actual filming found me standing atop the Empire State Building, staring down with wonderment at the city itself. My only prop was a visitor's map, featuring a cover shot of the Statue of Liberty and a brightly colored, oversized legend. "Let's get her looking vulnerable," I heard the director tell his crew, and for just a moment then, as I suddenly contemplated the distance beyond the reach of my fingertips, I was homesick.

So much so that as Sherry and I taped the interview portion of the film, I lost all sense of discretion. When she asked what was happening back in Tahlequah, I proceeded to share all the Tahlequah stories I could think of, even the salacious ones.

Later, as I was heading from the interview to the airport —in my rain cap—I stopped by a payphone to call Ginger and Mary with all the details of what I'd said on camera. At first, they thought I was joking, but soon they understood the seriousness of what I was telling them. Within a few days they wrote me a letter noting that, even though screening such films was not their usual practice, they were making an exception in my case.

*During World War II a Tahlequah jeweler who'd never
traveled outside the country before led his squadron
into a remote European village and recognized every
place he had ever been. Somehow, he'd instinctively
known where the bakery was, where the school was,
where the magistrate's office was. It was as if, he said,
Tahlequah had become the entire world and everything
he'd grown up with was just around the street corner.*

Remnants of Glory was officially released in 1981, when
I was twenty-eight years old, and I was alternately thrilled
and humbled by the experience. First of all, the novel didn't
turn out to be the unqualified critical success and permanent ticket to New York I'd anticipated. Though it had
received nice reviews in *Kirkus, Publisher's Weekly, Library
Journal,* and several nationally recognized newspapers, I
was still fixated on my one detractor, a critic in the *Denver
Post,* who'd described the dialogue as "leaden and pedantic."

It had also become increasingly apparent to me—and the
family—that nothing, not even the sale of paperback rights
to Berkeley and miniseries interest from the likes of David
Susskind, was going to warrant my hasty pledge to donate
half of all my gross proceeds to charity.

And then, thanks to an influx of reader mail, I'd discovered an irrevocable mistake in the text itself, missed by
myself and four sets of copyeditors. In a supposed-to-be
poignant scene between Kate and her sister Nona, the two
women were cleaning fish as they discussed the uncertain
future of Kate's retarded child. The editorial department had
asked me for more telling detail—which, I fantasized, was
my strong suit—and I'd transformed *fish* to *catfish* with just
a few inspired strokes from my typewriter. I'd even pointed
out the telltale scales on Kate's and Nona's unwashed hands.

But catfish don't have scales, and I have the postcards to

prove it. I was so traumatized by the revelation that I began frantically calling marine biologists and slightly inebriated fishermen throughout the country, hoping that someone, anyone could at least point out a mutant strain of catfish with scale-like appendages. Ultimately, I had to own the error of my words.

The more significant self-realization for me, though, bigger than catfish, which were just "red herrings," was that I had developed a very serious phobia about speaking in public, to the extent that I would be paralyzed for weeks in advance of any engagement. Not that I was slated for an extended book promotion. My itinerary was sporadic and mostly limited to Oklahoma—Pryor, Westville, and Tulsa. Only my one excursion into Fayetteville, Arkansas, delayed by two months, gave Grandma and me license to refer to these trips as a "summer-long regional tour."

The appearances usually just consisted of a brief talk, followed by a book signing, but none of them were small or disorganized enough to give me comfort. True, I could fly to New York and perform before strangers as Blanche Dubois. I just got "beside myself," as Grandma would say, when it came to doing stand-up presentations as an author.

I received all sorts of suggestions about how to address my fears, including the old standby, imagining that everyone in the audience was naked, but nothing scared me more than the prospect of looking out upon such a gathering. One amateur psychologist even suggested that perhaps I personally felt naked or exposed, since we've all had those dreams about suddenly realizing we're nude in the checkout line at Super-Saver. But I'm convinced the problem had more to do with remembering myself in those brown jumpers Grandma had given me with such high expectations, because a generation before they'd looked so cute on Mother. I still needed to develop a style of my own.

One of my old professors—the woman Grandma Miller

had met clandestinely at the Wagon Wheel—tried to help me rise above these feelings of inadequacy by booking me for one of her literary conferences that would also feature the visiting authors Edward Albee, Howard Nemerov, and Justin Kaplan. Almost any young novelist would have been intimidated by that lineup, but adding to my stress and distress, the Tahlequah newspaper ran pictures of all of us with the headline, *Pulitzer Winners to Speak at Northeastern.* Almost immediately, Mark and several others called to exclaim that they'd never realized I'd actually won the Pulitzer.

By the day of the event, I was so nervous that the conference director had to force-lead me on stage, but I somehow managed to stutter my way through the reading, lapsing only as Justin Kaplan and his wife, novelist Anne Bernays, slipped from the audience halfway through my presentation. Sure I had offended their literary sensibilities, I froze until Grandma Miller, who hadn't been invited, caught my attention from the doorway and willed me to continue.

Later that evening, Anne explained that she and Justin had only left because of conflicting schedules, and we chatted over drinks. She was the first novelist I had ever met in person, except for my brief encounter with Eudora Welty, and she was very supportive, visiting with me about everything from authorial voice to writer's block. When she returned to Boston, she mailed me a lapel pen, a totem eye, that I wore during several upcoming events, my way of channeling a continuum of women writers who could stare down any group.

Another novelist, Elizabeth Forsythe Hailey, who'd written the international best seller *A Woman of Independent Means,* had been kind enough to write a blurb for the novel. I felt a special connection with Betsy even before I'd met her, because while reading her book, told in letters, I'd suddenly known intuitively that her character Bess, based on her grandmother, and I shared the same birth date. Sure enough, as I turned the page to the next letter, dated November 23, Bess noted that it was her birthday, confirming this coincidental link between us.

I also received a surprise letter from legendary author and literary guru John Gardner (*The Art of Fiction*), who had chanced upon my book in New York and liked it, "very much." Without anticipating the eighteen-year-long writer's block that was ahead of me, he passed along the advice that I shouldn't feel rushed to complete a second novel. He wrote, "Let me suggest this: One of the things wrong with contemporary novels is that their authors don't sit on them long enough." Little did he know that I would carry his suggestion to the extreme; I'd always been an overachiever.

∽

During the eighteenth century Washington Irving, author of "The Legend of Sleepy Hollow" and "Rip Van Winkle," wrote about his travels through Oklahoma in A Tour on the Prairies. *Lest anyone expect too much from the frontier—or his fanciful literary reputation— he cautioned: "It is a simple narrative of every-day occurrences; such as happen to every one who travels the prairies."*

∽

To avoid having to give author talks or readings, I began to master the art of "drop-by" signings, simply showing up at stores unannounced and offering to sign any copies of *Remnants* that were in stock. I was operating under the illusion that if the books were autographed, bookstores couldn't return them to the publisher. Part of my strategy involved having Grandma in tow, because I'd discovered it was much harder for store managers to resist me if I introduced them to Grandma and hinted that the book was based on her life. Since she knew I was running low on resources—financially and creatively—she didn't seem to object if I *storied* a little.

We were experiencing a not-so-subtle shift in our relationship, for I'd become the undisputed person behind the wheel and was beginning to set off my own safety buzzers. Grandma had even helped me get a used car—a nondescript Mercury. Not that she was about to relegate herself to passenger status, compliantly squirming within the contours of a bucket seat. She still had plenty of advice for me, particularly after I'd honored my pledge to share my book proceeds by making a large donation to the Salvation Army. "I don't know how to tell you this, honey," she said, "but in an effort to unburden others, you've become a burden yourself."

And I had to be equally, but lovingly, uncompromising with her when I finally told her it wasn't safe for her to drive anymore. She argued with me at first, reminding me that she'd been driving for more than fifty years, starting with a stick shift and a hand-cranked engine. But then she relented, feeling the full force of her years and squinting, not just to see, but to understand. Of course I promised to take her as far as she wanted to go, but it would never be the same for her, for us, and she knew it. Her regrets weren't just for herself. She was anxious for me, too. She knew how lonely the road could be.

Remnants of Glory had covered nearly a century in heroine Kate Dexter's life, beginning with Oklahoma statehood. The time-span had been challenging for me, because I'd had to develop transitions from one era of Kate's story to the next. Grandma had given me a suggestion: "Why don't you say, 'And the next seven years passed smoothly?'" I explained that it just wasn't that easy to fast-forward fiction.

Ironically, though, *Remnants of Glory* did seem to accelerate the passage of time in our own lives. Grandma and I made one last trip together—to nowhere in particular—and headed into Tahlequah from the south, so she could savor her favorite view of the town. "Can you believe Mark's already been married?" she said, gazing into the distance, then adding, "And divorced." Mark's young son, Jonathan, had just been to visit, and his steady progress, as measured against the height tree etched into her closet door, made us even more aware of how quickly the days were slipping from us.

So I slowed down, and that's when she made her confession. She'd always wanted to go to Hawaii; she'd just never found the right time. It was a critical juncture for us—Grandma and I had traveled farther than I'd realized. "That's why you should go to all those places you've read about," she said. "Write about them yourself. Just be sure to . . ." She didn't need to finish. I understood. Our personal landmarks—those Oklahoma clearings she'd pointed out to me—would help me find her and myself again.

For a time, though, it became hard for us to recognize each other. An undiagnosed illness, complicated by severe anemia, made the world all but anonymous to Grandma, and she began introducing me as one of her friend's daughters—or even as Mother herself. Essentially, I'd evolved into a symbolic daughter, someone who could make intimate chores less embarrassing for her after she was bedfast, but not a woman she knew by name—or through shared life experience.

And for my part, I had trouble acknowledging the transformation in her. Doctors had done a bone-marrow biopsy checking for leukemia, which proved negative, but she'd uncharacteristically refused any further tests—and the steroid treatments that could have elevated her blood count. For all intents and purposes, Grandma had decided to die as ambiguously as Mother.

Our final days together were spent listening to books on tape, supplied by the National Library for the Blind. We even got to hear a recording of *Remnants*, which triggered her memories of her father's stallion, Rabitjoie, and of a tornado she'd once seen in western Oklahoma. But these remembrances were short-lived, and mostly the novel highlighted the stark contrast between fiction and real life, at least for me. Kate had been able to rebel against old age and escape from the nursing home. There was no escape for Grandma, restless in her bed, reaching out aimlessly for imaginary controls—a steering wheel, a pen, a skillet, anything that would make her feel useful again.

Only the refrains from poets she'd studied as a girl seemed to soothe her. We listened to them all—Emerson, Thoreau, Bryant—some on tape, some read by me, and their lyrics became our only conversation. Many times I had heard her quote Bryant's "Thanatopsis." The closing lines resonated with her and eventually with me: "sustained and soothed / By an unfaltering trust, approach thy grave, / Like one who wraps the drapery of his couch / About him, and lies down to pleasant dreams."

And that's how Grandma, who had traveled so extensively throughout the plains states, quietly passed away.

∽

My grandparents rarely all got together in the same car without us, but they did crowd into Grandma's Buick one Sunday afternoon to drop Mark and me off at Wesley's so we could meet our newest stepmother. As the Buick pulled away, they looked back and waved slightly—Grandma Crane even took her eyes off the road for a minute and tooted her horn; Grandpa Miller tipped his cowboy hat; Grandpa Crane ducked at a pretend right cross; and Grandma Miller dangled her scarf out the window like a conqueror's flag. Now they are gone, except for the tricks that memory plays, convincing me somehow that their journey continues.

∽

Shortly after Grandma's death, Mark stopped by the house one weekend for "no particular reason." I'd heard—the entire community had heard—that he was deeply involved with drugs, not only as a user but also as a manufacturer. But this wasn't the time for an intervention. He was too disheveled, immaculately dressed but emotionally ill clad with all the different guises that had fallen to us in grief. He'd more than done his part fielding the condolences with me, but we were both too weary from the emotional subterfuge to do more than stare at each other.

Grandma had left me her house, and he surveyed the living room searching for reminders, finally settling on the bookshelves she'd lined with photos instead of great novels. It was against that backdrop that he stood out for me, his real-life image seemingly insinuated among studio portraits of Grandma, Wesley, and Mother. He had Wesley's black-brown hair, Grandma's blue eyes, Mother's arched brows. And this was the enigma: he favored them all so much they even looked like each other. I wanted to tell him that and more, but the phone was ringing, and he rose to leave, pressured suddenly to say what had been burdening him. "Now that Grandma's gone," he declared, straddling the threshold, "there's nobody left who really cares what happens to us."

"But that's not so . . . ," I tried to reassure him, except I couldn't finish. I hadn't even been able to write Grandma's obituary, because I'd temporarily lost my voice—and not just as a writer. Perhaps, like Grandpa Crane, I was choking on everything I'd always wanted to say. So even after Mark left, I sat silenced behind the sky-blue typewriter Grandpa had surprised me with once while I was in college. I kept a blank sheet of paper in at all times—just in case the words started to come again.

In the meantime, I was making a patchwork living by teaching as an adjunct at Flaming Rainbow University (a street school) in Stilwell, Northeastern State University in Tahlequah, and Rogers State College in Claremore, all so far removed from each other that I seemed to spend more time on the road than I did at home in Grandma's old house.

The Mercury Grandma had gotten me had become a metaphor without her—sort of a secondhand car-of-life with a four-year note and worn-out shock absorbers. I wanted to fill it with other people; I even tried to make a passenger out of Wesley, but the Mercury was no place for us to begin transacting a relationship. During one of our outings, he feigned illness at Jonathan's birthday party in Arkansas, and a group of men, who told us they'd been disappointed by early departures in their own lives, helped him into the car and secured his safety belt. After all, they reminded us, most accidents happened close to home, so it wasn't as if we hadn't been forewarned that we might be headed for a collision of some sort, even if it was just with each other.

Once we were finally on the road, Wesley "napped" in the backseat, the way he'd done during our trips for his radiation treatments, but he began to show remarkable resilience as soon as we approached his driveway. That's when he gave himself away by suddenly blurting that, thank goodness, he'd gotten back just in time to see the Sooners kick off on national television.

How did Harper Lee spend her weekends? I wondered, as I threw the car into gear before he could escape and circled Tahlequah proper for a furious two hours, extending our drive an extra fifteen minutes every time he tried to justify himself. He'd meant well, he said, by concealing Mother's death, then shielding my stepmother after she'd beaten me. And he truly loved football—it was his release—though he'd never thrown a pass in his life.

When I finally did relent and let him out at his front door, well into the third quarter, he swore that he would never ride with me again and parted company by declaring that I sounded "awfully leaden and pedantic" to him.

We'd logged over three hundred miles together that

afternoon, driving everywhere but nowhere. And—this was the hard part—I was on the same meandering course professionally. Sometimes, usually when I was stuck behind a hay baler on Highway 82 to Claremore, I'd pull one of Grandma's maps from the glove compartment, stretch its accordion folds to the limit, and hope that its legend—one inch equaled one hundred miles—might keep my faraway dreams in perspective.

New York, according to Texaco, was only six feet to the east, but getting there a third time, by the measure of my own words, was going to be the trickiest trip of all. Particularly since the first line of my new novel, "For the moment Marie only wanted to see the fair . . .," dropped off into the same void where I was still tracking down catfish.

I continued to maintain ties with my East Coast friends, and Sherry, who'd become a pioneer in audio publishing, sent me free books on tape to help me make the most of my commute to various jobs. As I sped around trailer rigs, school buses, and "seniors on wheels," I'd be listening to Anne Tyler's *Dinner at the Homesick Restaurant*—I was hungry—and Anne Rice's *Interview with a Vampire*—I was scared. I spent a whole week riding with Raymond Carver, another with Sue Grafton. Sherry's authors and I experienced the world together, and I grew impatient with any distractions that reminded me that I was in Oklahoma again, bypassing an Amish farm home with a phone booth in the front yard. The occupants, it seemed, didn't believe in indoor phones.

One afternoon I got stuck behind a family bulging from the cab of a pickup truck, barely up to cruising speed at twenty miles per hour—in a no-passing zone. The more I honked, the more they smiled and waved back at me. Then I saw their bumper sticker: *Honk If You Love Jesus.* They'd mistaken my frustration for affirmation; we were going the same way but thinking in different directions. That's how we traveled the next forty miles and before long, despite myself, I began to catch glimpses of Grandma in the clearings. The road can do that to you.

⌒

When I was in sixth grade, my teacher, who'd traveled to desert places around the world, brought back what he called a "relief map" of the Southwest, though he explained that "relief" wasn't what we typically thought of as comfort. "This isn't a map of all the best ice cream stands," he told us, "but of the natural terrain, in 3-D, so you can get a feel for any obstacles before you take to the back roads or start out on foot." Accordingly, the map's legend highlighted wilderness areas, hills, valleys—their density, their elevations, their depths. So this was a very different perspective of travel, but one to keep in mind if journeys became complicated.

⌒

One night when I got home late, Wesley's Lincoln was idling in front of the house, and he asked me to get in with him so we could talk. He was driving with one foot on the gas, the other on the brake, as if he were at odds with himself, but he finally broke and told me the news. Mark, who'd become such an accomplished attorney in his own right, had been arrested for drug trafficking, though he was out on bail, at least for the time being. To complicate matters, multiple charges were still pending, and Mark wouldn't commit to rehab, so this was serious. As always, Wesley was impeccably dressed in a Hickey Freeman suit, offset with one of his trademark red ties. But he was clearly shaken and had accidentally turned on his emergency flashers.

"It's not like this comes as a surprise exactly," I said. Only a few weeks before I'd gotten a midnight call from Jonathan, telling me that, much to his delight, he and Mark had just driven through a police stakeout without anyone recognizing them.

But Wesley *had* been caught off guard—he was that single-minded, focusing so exclusively on his work sometimes that he often failed to understand life in a larger context. Earlier that year, he'd hurried out to Wal-Mart to buy the cheapest music cassettes he could find for the enhanced "hold" feature on his answering machine. Without realizing it, he'd picked up a Tina Turner tape, and his clients had been listening to "What's Love Got to Do with It" for several weeks before a local CPA called it to his attention.

"I'll try to talk to Mark, too," I said, but my words didn't sound genuine, even to me, and I wasn't optimistic for any of us.

Neither was Wesley. He'd instinctively driven to the courthouse, but he corrected course, and we spent the rest of the evening circumventing other worry zones—the jail, the hospital, and the cemetery. Then we broadened our route to bypass Grandma Miller's old house—the new owners had let it go—and the doctor's office. Small-town driving can be that tricky when you're trying to elude your personal history at every street corner.

"Do you hear the racket?" Wesley said, rolling down his window, as if inviting some sort of healthy clamor into our lives, that raucousness of words misspoken but still heartfelt.

"No," I said, but I understood his desperation on such a quiet evening. We been fooled, all of us, into thinking there was some sort of etiquette that could hush the darkness.

So we listened to Larry King on talk radio and kept driving. It was after midnight when we wound up in front of the Methodist Church, the one where Wesley had married Mother, such a joyful occasion that even Grandma Crane had approved of the union, based on Wesley's history as a loyal Democrat. The old church wasn't nearly as grand as the upscale version—with its spires and steeples—but the memories there helped us find a way home.

But is there for the night a resting place?
    A roof for when the slow dark hours begin.

—Christina Rossetti, "Up-Hill"

My grandmothers always insisted that Mark and I accompany them every Decoration/Memorial Day to visit all the final resting places of our not-to-be-forgotten relatives. We had so many to remember that ours was a circuitous journey. Our point of origin, of course, was Tahlequah, but we drove as far afield as the Civil War battlefield in Prairie Grove, Arkansas, where we honored our fallen soldiers with homemade flower baskets, then indulged ourselves with picnic lunches of fried chicken. So Decoration Day was a full-fledged holiday, a kind of after-party for the departed that comforted us with notions that we'd eventually be remembered with just as much festivity.

One day, though, when I was in junior high school, some friends and I were playing softball on the campus and noticed that we'd kicked up enough dirt to expose a smooth slate surface we could use as a permanent home plate. As we dropped to our knees to brush away another layer of debris, we inadvertently exposed a name, withheld here out of respect, and the dates, 1825–1840, which noted the passage of a young girl's life.

At first, we just exchanged anxious glances, but then we dug more furiously, even using our bats to loosen the ground. For suddenly we had a new pastime, which had nothing to do with building a softball diamond—or excavating history. We were digging to convince ourselves that our own lives were significant—that if a young girl, about our age, did get swallowed up by the earth itself, she would resurface again, even in play.

The next day, more of our friends became involved, and we found two more tombstones, a family cluster, before our science teacher intervened and confirmed that we had, indeed, happened upon an old cemetery. Then she advised us not to disturb the dead, to respect their lives by living our own. We still tried to adorn the graves with jonquils, but eventually a new generation of topsoil overtook our handiwork, and we began playing softball again—on the kind of sacred ground that was our discreet foundation.

Sacred Ground

*An Indian healer and master fisherman lived on Lake
Tenkiller—in a cove naturally secluded by the Cookson
Hills and the uneven bend of the lake itself. If you had
an ailment, all you had to do was meet him there,
and he would lay his hand on your infirmities with
confidence. Some people claimed that the setting itself
was magical, but those who had journeyed down the
two-lane highway and walked the narrow path to this
man's trailer knew—from the very weight of their
afflictions—that it was his human touch, native and
unyielding, that sanctified such a remote place.*

෴

Mark's arrest made the front page of all the local and
even the regional newspapers. Wesley didn't respond directly, but he suddenly revolted by abandoning his own
strict dress code and wearing Bermuda shorts—with
trouser-length socks, including garters—almost every
weekend. He also confounded everyone by buying sneakers
to go with his business suits, prompting one of our cousins
to explain, "He's secretly relieved, and he just can't hide it
anymore. As much as he hates the idea of having Mark in
prison, he's hoping the law will somehow save him."

What she said was true for all of us, because Mark, who
was claiming innocence by reason of entrapment, absolutely refused to acknowledge that he had a problem with
drugs, though he hadn't shown up for work in months and
Wesley, as his partner, had been left with the added responsibility of taking on his caseload. We'd even confronted
Mark with evidence: his briefcase filled with bags of marijuana, his garage equipped with expensive growing lights
and lined with rows of marijuana plants.

But Mark, brilliant as he was, didn't want to talk facts. He
wanted to talk philosophy: *Didn't Wesley himself rely on prescription sedatives? And didn't people have all sorts of different hobbies?* At one point, after Wesley suggested *fishing* as

an alternative, Mark actually threatened to report *us* to the police for breaking and entering. We were guilty as charged, but only because we were afraid he'd overdosed on more dangerous drugs, such as methamphetamines, which we'd heard were a particular weakness.

In fact we became so suspect in his eyes that when he was caught on videotape outside the Leflore County Courthouse, allegedly accepting "meth" as payment for a case, he initially accused us of tipping off authorities. But we'd never considered such a betrayal—even for his own good. We didn't want him arrested; we wanted him helped. Wesley immediately got him a noted defense attorney, who arranged to have him released on bail so Mark could enter a drug treatment program. However, even the possibility of a prison sentence wasn't enough to strong-arm him into rehab. He checked himself out of the Tulsa clinic after only twenty-four hours and went on the lam—not from the authorities, since his official hearing wouldn't be for weeks, but from the family.

Ultimately it took one of Wesley's lady companions, not a Tulsa therapist, to point out why Mark was so unreachable. He didn't have a mother or anyone else in his life who was close enough to appeal to him on a deeper level. Of course, he adored Jonathan, but we couldn't expect a child, still in grade school, to rehabilitate his father.

The only other person Mark had loved unconditionally was one of his ex-wives, who'd cheated on him with a mutual acquaintance, reported him to authorities, and physically assaulted him. Even after she abandoned him, he continued to send her flowers, hoping for a reconciliation. When Wesley finally asked him what it was about this woman that appealed to him so much, he said he liked her personality.

We *did* have one legal recourse, which was to have Mark declared incompetent, but Wesley refused to consider that option. He couldn't humiliate him in that way. Besides, when given a forum, no one could be more articulate than Mark—the reason he'd been such an accomplished attorney before deciding to forgo due process and personally repeal any laws that didn't accommodate his own lifestyle. A competency hearing would likely rebound in his favor, declaring him of sound mind and making him all the more liable for his actions.

So we waited, hoping for some sort of last-minute reprieve, not from the state, but from this addiction—or need—which was holding us all captive.

✺

On May 2, 1920, a deadly tornado ripped through the small community of Peggs, Oklahoma, and killed seventy-one people who were caught by surprise. One man, who was lucky enough to survive, was actually picked up by the funnel before being dropped back to earth to confront the loss of his family and friends. Today Peggs thrives as a highway town on SH 82. People drive through on their way to Tulsa and beyond, often stopping at one of its convenience stores, where they enjoy their sodas and hot dogs without even drawing a deep breath of remembrance—or considering the need for shelters in their own lives.

✺

I was still traveling from school to school, but I developed a special bond with Flaming Rainbow University in Stilwell, the most unique stop on my route. Targeting first-generation college students, "The Flame," as we called it, featured a fully accredited four-year curriculum and brought together the most diverse group of people I'd ever met—under less than ideal circumstances. Our "campus" was, in everyday parlance, a dilapidated warehouse, ventilated by broken glass—and broken dreams.

Accordingly, *Flaming Rainbow*, a mythic symbol of

regeneration in Native American literature, became a very different sort of metaphor for these job-seeking students, whose vision quests had already been compromised by reality. Ironically, the closest any of them had ever come to receiving a life bonus was when, a few years earlier, Mark had represented one couple in a malpractice suit involving a child born with club feet. They'd lost the case, though they didn't blame Mark, and had been scrambling ever since to survive on a subsistence living. Their subsequent expectations were meager: they hoped that by getting degrees they'd someday be able to provide quality medical care for their three children.

And the other students revealed goals through their essays that were just as lofty in their simplicity. They were saving for refrigerators so their staples would last longer; they were raising gardens so they could supplement their meals; and they were committing crimes, mostly petty theft, so they'd never have to steal again. At first their revelations frightened me. I was driving back and forth to Stilwell in the dark and would often spot cars with smashed windshields in the dim neon light outside our building. But one night a young woman waited behind to reassure me that, as their teacher, I didn't have to worry. The class was protecting me, and before long I even began to feel an extended sense of security outside their jurisdiction.

It was their writing—with my feedback—that was initiating the conversations between us and establishing our unlikely kinship. Though our textbooks were generic—relying on traditional essay formats—my Rainbow friends continued to overreach the margins of their assignments by writing frankly from the breadth of real-life experience. A middle-aged student turned a "how-to" essay into a riveting commentary on poverty by telling how she targeted garage sales in wealthier neighborhoods, sorting through trash cans immediately after the events, because people of means tended to discard unsold items rather than box them up for charities.

Another older woman stood before us and read her account of being gang-raped outside a Los Angeles movie theater, a random act with very predictable results—she'd felt isolated and afraid ever since and had returned home to Stilwell to find solace in familiar surroundings. As she shared her story—very forthrightly—I could feel the class closing ranks around her. Not only had she entrusted them enough to let her guard down; she'd also given them a peculiar sense of privilege. For despite their impoverished circumstances—Stilwell was one of the poorest towns in Oklahoma—they were living in a place someone regarded as a safe haven.

Not all their essays were so emotionally wrenching, particularly as Christmas approached and they began sharing their favorite holiday stories and dilemmas. A girl in her early twenties, recently married, explained that she'd always spent most of her Christmas fund on those closest to her, but this year she was making an exception. She felt so guilty for disliking her pesky mother-in-law that she was being more generous with her than anyone else, even her new husband, and this made her heartsick.

Since the class was so strapped financially, I didn't want to make anyone uncomfortable by suggesting a group celebration, but I did bring cookies for our final meeting before the holidays. Much to my surprise, though, every one of the students brought presents to me—as the teacher presiding over their aspirations. I'd never received such bounty—candles from unemployed young people who didn't have electricity, chocolate-covered peanuts from parents who didn't know if they could log enough extra hours at the canning factory to buy frozen turkeys. And then the most telling gift of all, a delicately embroidered Christmas card, featuring a cardinal beneath the hand-stitched banner—GREETINGS—from the woman who'd been sexually assaulted.

We got to spend only one more semester together. The school, grant-funded, was on the verge of bankruptcy, and more times than not I didn't receive my monthly check. So I'd made the hard decision to take out a mortgage on Grandma's house so I could devote more time to the new novel and work my way into a permanent teaching position at Rogers State College in Claremore.

At least I had options, a fact I came to appreciate even more the night a tornado siren sounded during class, and we huddled together in the hall, hoping as a group that the funnel wouldn't inadvertently target Flaming Rainbow. All of us who'd grown up in Tornado Alley knew that a hallway was always the shelter of last resort, so we tried to ward off this particular tornado by recalling the capriciousness of other storms—how clothes racks, lined with perfectly hung dresses, had been discovered in the midst of devastated storefronts. How family albums, open to favorite snapshots, had been recovered—in pristine condition—from the rubble of collapsed homes. Eventually we did get the all-clear, but even then we paused briefly to examine ourselves, to sift through the debris of our imaginations and celebrate our joint good fortune at being spared.

It was that same sense of community that carried me through to the end of the semester, when I said my good-byes and, simultaneously, acknowledged these students for the first time. Suddenly I remembered how baffled I'd been when several of them had missed class after Lucille Ball's death. I'd confronted one man, who'd patiently explained that I just didn't realize how much Lucy had meant to them—she'd made everyone laugh. And even as I drove away that last evening and caught a glimpse of the class waving in my rearview mirror, I recalled how, in the beginning, I'd fussed at them over grammar and punctuation. As if a comma could make the difference in someone's life and Lucy couldn't.

∾

After Wesley married my stepmother Louise, who was his true life-partner, they made annual summer visits to see her family in Wilmette, Illinois. But he always managed to work in two side trips: one to Waukegan, hometown of Jack Benny, a place, he said, that was so understated that it, "well," made him smile. Even the traffic lights, he claimed, had perfect timing. The other spot was the Biograph Theater in downtown Chicago, where Dillinger was shot. "Allegedly," Wesley emphasized, because the subterfuge of history—and laughter—was what intrigued him so much.

∿

Since I was essentially unemployed except for part-time teaching stints, I hadn't been able to get much of a mortgage on Grandma's house, but I did put enough money together to make a trip to New York with no other goal in mind than reaffirming my literary friendships and reconnecting with myself as a writer. It was in New York, after all, where I'd first been recognized beyond the small town distinctions of being Wesley's daughter, Grandma's designated driver, and the original concept person behind "About Tahlequah."

Even after six years, *Remnants of Glory* was still my "letter of transit" into the New York literary world, but after I arrived and continued to ward off questions about the book-in-progress, I soon realized that stand-alone novels had limited cachet. Nevertheless, Mary and Ginger were enormously supportive and arranged for me to go with them to the airport to pick up their star client, Alice Munro. As one of Alice's first editors, Sherry had been able to send me complimentary copies of her early work, and I'd read and reread *The Beggar Maid* and *The Progress of Love*, books

that clearly established Alice as one of the most commanding writers of the twentieth century.

In person, though, wielding her own suitcase and speculating about the latest tabloid headlines, she was remarkably
down-to-earth—and unaffected by her own notoriety. On
the ride back to Ginger's brownstone, she had mentioned
Remnants to Alice, and by the time we'd gotten together
later that evening for drinks, Alice had started reading the
book and told me how much the setting and overall atmosphere reminded her of rural Canada. In other words, she
recognized a lost writer when she saw one and was extending the equivalent of a creative handshake.

That same generosity of spirit came through the next evening at the 92nd Street YWCA, after she'd delivered a stunning reading of her short story "Lichen" that was followed
by an autograph session. As Alice greeted her fans—they
were legion—she noticed that I'd slipped off to the side-
lines, and she motioned for me to join her at the signing
table so we could "visit."

The highlight of the trip came the following day when
Mary and I spent the morning with Alice in SoHo helping
her find an outfit to wear for an appearance she was making
at Harvard. Again, as she sorted through the possibilities,
all of them classic cuts, I was struck by her artful simplicity. Eventually she settled on a finely beaded, antique dress,
measuring it against her image in the mirror and instinctively knowing it was right.

Earlier Mary had explained the significance of SoHo as
an arts district, but by the time Alice I parted company after
lunch, it had begun to feel more like a special province in
Canada with open borders. For somehow Alice had learned
about my grandmother's death, and after sharing insights
about her own mother's passing, she hugged me with one
last piece of advice: I was trying to come to terms with too
much too soon.

I *was* restless—Alice was right about that—and when I got back to Tahlequah, still unable to locate myself behind the typewriter, I decided to embark on one more, almost desperate, literary outing, this time to visit a writer friend in Virginia. Sherry had sent me a biography of author Caroline Gordon, who'd been able to write extensively during a bus trip. So I decided that I should emulate Gordon, take the Greyhound to Lexington, and let the rhythm of the road become the tempo for my narrative.

But by the time we rolled into the Nashville depot at midnight, I was the only woman on the bus and my writing tablets had become nothing more than excess baggage. As soon as I could get to a pay phone, I called a local book critic who'd always told me to let him know if I was ever in town. Clearly I'd taken him by surprise, but he and his groggy wife picked me up at the station, put me up for the night, and packed me a picnic lunch for the rest of my journey.

The return trip was eventful in another way. Several passengers, just released from prison, were caught smoking pot, and the exasperated driver declared that he'd chauffeured busloads of teenagers who were more civilized. Luckily, I'd cozied up to a professional softball player, Harry, who shielded us with his bat. A regular on the route, Harry told me all sorts of lore about competitive passengers who'd broken records for the most consecutive days on the road.

Two past champions, both middle-aged women who'd been bus-bound for over a week, were sitting just across from us. When I finally took leave of them in Ft. Smith, Arkansas, they applauded, knowing they had outlasted yet another passenger. I'd seen them earlier as they'd sorted through their "carry-on bags," which I suspected contained most of their worldly belongings. That's when I began to understand the secret to their road success. They didn't have a place to go and just hoped to distinguish themselves in their confusion.

Ft. Smith, by the way, was the closest connection I could get to Tahlequah by bus, since we no longer had a depot. As one of our local proprietors had explained once, no one got to Tahlequah by accident. But our mistakes often kept us there.

❧

In Lexington, Virginia, tourists regularly visit the recumbent statue of General Robert E. Lee that immortalizes him asleep in the aftermath of historic turmoil. In fact many homes in Virginia—throughout the South—have attained museum status because noted personages have rested within their walls. Their repose is commemorated with memorial plaques affixed to the houses themselves. It's as if sleep, a simple act of trust and abandon, can sanctify even an ordinary place forever.

❧

Curiously, even though *Remnants* was known as a book without a sequel throughout the rest of the country, it was just starting to catch on in Tahlequah. A local newspaper even established a whole new category—"Favorite Writer"—for its annual reader poll, which also highlighted the most popular restaurants, car washes, and dog grooming salons in the community.

As the designated Favorite Writer three years in a row, I was regularly called upon to host literary guests who were speaking at Northeastern State College. I always enjoyed these brief encounters and was especially thrilled when asked to show Pulitzer-winning novelist Alison Lurie around town. My hope was to present Lurie and another guest writer with copies of *Remnants*. Though the book was out-of-print, I was relieved when a Tulsa book dealer told me over the phone that she did, indeed, have two hardcover copies, one ten dollars, the other twenty-five. "Is the ten-dollar book damaged in some way?" I asked. But she quickly explained that the more expensive book had been signed by the author. Never mind that I *was* the author. I ended up having to pay an extra fifteen dollars for my own signature.

I did get a chance to speak with Lurie briefly about my writer's block. She told me not to fret so much, that she sometimes worried that if she wrote too *many* novels, critics wouldn't take her as seriously. But mostly she was interested in talking about Tahlequah, and as we walked the length of Main Street, I pointed out as many historical landmarks as I could, including my personal favorite, the Cherokee National Capitol in the center of the courthouse square.

But Lurie's focus had shifted across the street to Shrimp's pawnshop, just the kind of place, she told me, where she could cap off the afternoon and buy souvenirs for her friends back in New York. My heart was beating out exclamation points, because just a few weeks before, I'd been forced to put Grandma Miller's silver tea service on sale with Shrimp, and I knew he would call it to our attention. "But it's closed!" I blurted, even though Shrimp himself was waving at us, and she was headed right for him.

Once we were inside, I kept trying to signal Shrimp to keep quiet, but just as we were about to make a clean get-away, he announced that he'd finally sold my silver, "for less than it was worth," but he knew how desperate I was for some cash. So much for my big plans to impress Lurie. She regarded me with justifiable suspicion after Shrimp's revelation.

Just a few nights after Lurie's visit, I had my first money-related nightmare, dreaming I'd gone to Wal-Mart and found Woody Allen working as a cashier in the express lane. When I asked him why he, a brilliant director, was holding down a job in the Tahlequah Wal-Mart, he replied, "Times

are rough for artists everywhere. This is nothing. Alice
Munro is the new hostess out at Tahlequah Motor Lodge."

❧

Even though the young adult novel Where the Red
Fern Grows *is set in Tahlequah, the movie version was
actually filmed near the Arkansas border, where set
directors could capture the feel of a smaller town, more
like Tahlequah before the advent of Wal-Mart and
McDonald's. So when we gathered for the local premier
in a downtown theater, tastefully decorated with red
plastic ferns, we frustrated ourselves by trying to anchor
the story in local landmarks. We all admitted that the
storefronts captured the look of Tahlequah in another
era, but the foliage was different, and as one woman
put it, a town can't seem real when it's east of itself.*

❧

I did—finally—get the full-time job I'd hoped for, teaching creative writing and composition at Rogers State College, which was more open than the local university to
accepting my novel in lieu of a doctor's degree. Claremore
was over ninety miles away, so the round-trip commute was
more than three hours, and my teaching load was heavy.
But the salary did cover my bills—almost—and I began
regaining some self-confidence. I even made progress on
the new novel, adding a final phrase to the opening line
and forming my first complete sentence: "For the moment
Marie only wanted to see the fair—*some people called it a
carnival.*"

Because I was on the road so much, it was hard for me to
keep track of myself, and sometimes I would return home
to discover that in my rush I'd forgotten to leave on the
front porch light to guide me safely into the house after
dark. One night, when I arrived late, I was startled to find
an empty glass on the kitchen counter and the toilet un-
flushed. To add to my concern, the back door, which I was

so sure I'd locked that morning, was ajar. I called the police, and together we surmised that someone, most likely a harmless itinerant, had slipped inside while I was retrieving the morning paper, then escaped out the back after I'd left for work.

At first I was uneasy about this invasion of my privacy, but I was so preoccupied with work, including my new radio show, that after a few days, I stopped double-checking the doors and began relegating any excess concerns to Post-it-note status, stockpiling memos to myself in clutter drawers that I'd set aside at home and at school.

One day, though, I received an anonymous package in the mail that did catch my attention—it had been addressed to me using a Rogers State parking decal. Inside I found some physics notes wrapped around a cassette tape, encased in an old Radio Shack calculator box and labeled with the stick-on letters "N Moment Carpe Diem" on one side and "BOTF in Time" on the other. And the tape itself was just as cryptic, one-line sound bites from approximately one hundred different songs, ranging from "Do You Know the Way to San Jose" to "Send in the Clowns."

After I played a portion of the tape for my colleague Penny, she reminded me that I'd received a similar package several months before, and sure enough I did find it stuffed into my file cabinet along with a companion poem about a mysterious troubadour. The first recording hadn't been as unsettling as the new tape—it had contained full-length songs by an amateur singer. I'd even fancied at one point that it might have been from a man I'd loved once who'd found a quirky way to stay in touch with me.

But "BOTF in Time" was serious. Penny, who had studied psychology as well as English, couldn't emphasize her concern enough, and so on her advice, our other colleague, Judy, and I took the tape to the Claremore police. Even as we pulled into the station parking lot, I was second-guessing myself—it was just a prank, nothing to merit official concern. And initially, John Cummings, the chief investigator, tended to downplay it as well, though he did promise to listen to it in its entirety—something we'd been unable to do, because it was so frenzied.

That evening I had to teach a late class, and it wasn't until I was on my way home that I called from my mobile phone to check my voicemail. John had already left a message. After listening to the tape, which had become increasingly violent, he had serious concerns for my safety and suspected that whoever had patched it together had been observing me on a regular basis. Of course, he wanted to follow up, but in the meantime, he urged me to be thinking of anyone who might target me in this way. Since Mark was still facing criminal charges, I wondered if the tape could somehow be related to his "trials," but I knew better. No one in my life was capable of such duplicity; this was the work of a stranger.

The night closed in on me then, and I was just as scared of oncoming headlights as I was of the darkness itself. I called ahead to my friend Lori and arranged for her and a local police officer to meet me at the house. The officer admitted he was afraid to make the first move and asked Lori and me to take the lead by unlocking the front door and switching on all the lights. When we did, when we saw Grandma smiling at us from the gallery of family photos, the world suddenly righted itself.

Just the week before, I'd enjoyed watching Whitney Houston and Kevin Costner in the stalker film *The Bodyguard*, scared only that I might run out of popcorn. Because women living in small towns, pursuing modest livings, and holding onto youthful dreams were never pursued so relentlessly. That sense of ordinariness steadied me, even when my new cat, Skylar, awakened me from the early morning quiet by rattling the blinds so convincingly.

∼

One of my cousins drove up from Oklahoma City to visit the family landmarks in Tahlequah, and we met in Grandpa's old furniture store, which had been converted into a bar, Ned's, with pool tables. But even as we sipped wine and listened to the jukebox, our memories were busy reconstructing life as it had once been, dinettes in the foyer, Hotpoint refrigerators beyond the coat racks. And from there it wasn't hard to imagine Grandpa himself, on duty at the valet stand as a kind of antithetical bouncer, quick to promise free deliveries and forgive his debtors.

~

On my way to work the next morning, I kept a careful watch on my rearview mirror and saw nothing more than the typical "wide loads" that usually crowded the narrow highway. It was winter, and I did need to slow down occasionally for patches of black ice. I also had to dodge an errant station wagon, with a "Pro Life" bumper sticker, that suddenly pulled in front of me and began swerving back and forth on the slick asphalt. But the wagon was loaded with kids drawing smiley faces on the steamed windows, so unless I was being stalked by an entire family, this was just homespun recklessness not directed at me personally.

John had asked me to try deciphering the labeling on the cassette, but except for the phrase, *carpe diem*, translation "seize the day," the letter combinations *BOTF* and other allusions didn't register with me. I even tried replaying the tape—at least the portions I'd listened to—in my mind's ear. I remembered a clip from "Secret Agent Man" and even a line from the movie *Cool Hand Luke*, "What we've got here is a failure to communicate," but again, I couldn't establish any personal connection. My convenient conclusion was that the tapes, the poem, and the physics notes had been sent to me by accident—a far-fetched explanation, I knew, but no more so than the stalker theory.

That would have been an easy assumption for John and his department, too, trained to investigate crimes that had already been committed, but within a few days they were back in touch. An outside psychologist had reviewed the tapes and agreed that the song excerpts were directed at me personally and became progressively violent, ending with one song lyric about shooting someone with a forty-five. The psychologist also shared John's opinion that whoever had spent so much time piecing the tapes together had more than likely been stalking me.

So suddenly, life for me wasn't just a matter of taking Sherry's advice and being discreet on the streets of Manhattan. I was going to have to be equally guarded at home. And, John cautioned, I would have to be more aware of my surroundings, which in my case, meant setting aside my big-city daydreams and resigning myself to the fact that for the time being I was going to have to focus on Oklahoma.

John had one other piece of news—withheld just long enough to help me ease into the scary reality of what we were facing. Through the physics notes enclosed with the last mailing, he'd identified a possible suspect. The notes had come from a Rogers State textbook that the professor had only used for one semester in a class with just a handful of students, one of whom was from Chouteau, where the last package had been postmarked. This same student, in his mid-thirties, had also been enrolled in back-to-back short-term courses I'd taught a few summers before at a satellite campus.

John had printed out the student's name for me along with his profile, neither of which jogged any memories. I'd been teaching a hundred-plus students a semester and often had trouble placing those who hadn't taken my classes on an ongoing basis. Anticipating this, the police department had kept an eye on the suspect for a day or two before pulling him over for an expired safety inspection sticker so a backup unit could get a surveillance shot of him and his car that might help me recognize him. But the photo didn't sharpen the fuzzy mental images I had of him. He was a nondescript white male with dark hair and wire-rimmed glasses, no one who stood out to me even routinely as I thought back through the past several months.

We did have one way of delving more deeply into the man's life, though John was the first to admit that it was risky and might even aggravate the situation, so the final call would be mine. The department could get a search warrant to check out the home where the suspect, who had no work history, was living with his mother. If he was indeed the one responsible for the threatening tapes, we'd tip our hand, but we might also intimidate him enough to keep the threats from escalating.

"Okay," I said finally, and just "okay" because I was still hoping to discover that we'd only been *storying* to ourselves and could soon officially dismiss the case as a false alarm.

The department executed the search a few days later, and John called to report the findings. The suspect had been operating out of his mother's attic, and it had provided just enough evidence to justify our concerns: unfinished letters addressed to me, more tapes in the process of being dubbed, two books on how to kill people, a pornographic film—and two loaded guns. Police had also found some drug paraphernalia and misdemeanor amounts of marijuana.

Though the suspect had at first denied anything more than sending the tapes to me in hopes of getting his work published, John challenged him on his anonymity, and he eventually admitted he had "a thing for me." He didn't elaborate, which squared with the physics professor's assessment that he was extremely bright. His actions and the evidence at hand might have implicated him, but his words were measured.

A few mornings later, as I was entering Claremore, I spotted the suspect's car at an intersection, and his eyes locked with mine so intently that I knew he'd been waiting for me. I called the police from my mobile phone, and, on the district attorney's advice, John encouraged me to get a protective order and cooperate with the DA in filing stalking charges. Though stalking had just been recognized as a crime in Oklahoma and the definition hadn't been legally tested, the overall feeling was that the charge itself—attached to real consequences—would act as a deterrent.

The following Friday the suspect was arrested on the Rogers State College campus, where he was still enrolled in a couple of classes. The police department called to share the good news, and I looked forward to my first relaxed weekend in a month. But that afternoon, as I entered the campus, I saw the suspect and an older woman picking up his car. John later confirmed that the stalker's mother, a registered nurse, had posted a thousand-dollar bond, and he'd been released into her custody.

Of course, John assured me that the charges themselves, the first stalking charges filed in Rogers County, were still in place. And authorities in his home county had filed misdemeanor drug charges against him, but the suspect was free for the time being and perhaps more agitated than ever. I kept referring to him as "the suspect," even though I knew his name. Because for me he'd become the scary equivalent of *Everyman*, personifying all our late-night suspicions about even the people closest to us, who frightened us sometimes by seeming like strangers.

Later that night, as I recalled seeing him and his mother leaving the campus together, I suddenly began to process the loss of my own mother on a more profound level. Grandma had always characterized her in such mythic terms that it had been hard for me to imagine her as a real presence to be missed in my life. Or at least that had been the case until I opened a bottle of pinot grigio and started rummaging through the cedar chest Grandma had packed with mothball remembrances, annotated in her finest hand.

In one note, stuffed inside Mother's baptismal Bible, Grandma (who'd feared she might not live long enough herself to pass along a spiritual legacy) tried to document Mother's angelic status and urged Mark and me to embrace religion in our own lives. She also used a longer letter, carefully folded inside Mother's diploma, to make an equally emotional argument for higher education.

But I made some interesting discoveries all on my own—a lipstick smudged valentine Mother had sent to Wesley; her for-real Social Security card; and a soup spoon buried inside her jewelry box, over-packed with bulky, colorful necklaces. The spoon was what intrigued me most; it made her human, a busy accountant/mother, who'd inadvertently included this emblem of everyday life in a case filled with her adornments.

I found some poems, too, about me, awkwardly rhymed but eloquent in their sincerity. Though my own words still eluded me, I'd learned something new about my character Marie that night—she didn't have a mother either.

∽

I once ran into my cousin at Six Flags Over Texas, the amusement center of the Southwest, but we didn't speak because we were teenagers on band trips and weren't able to recognize each other outside of established perimeters, even though we saw remarkable resemblances. It wasn't until later, when we met at Grandma's during Thanksgiving and stared out the window at her crooked magnolia tree, that we forgot all about Ferris wheels and became familiar to ourselves again.

∽

The next practical step for us was to get a protective order, which the district attorney's office thought would be nothing more than a routine procedure. Though I'd have to be sworn in and called to the witness stand, I'd only be asked to make a brief statement. I wouldn't even have to confront the suspect; he'd be represented by his attorney, who had agreed not to fight the order. The attorney had already called me at work to put me at ease by explaining that his client was just socially awkward. I, in turn, had professed my sympathy for a fellow human being who was so clearly troubled.

This spirit of cooperation was more than just a strategy— at least on my part. None of us were determined to see the suspect in jail, and I'd promised to drop the stalking charges if he would only submit to a psychiatric evaluation and adhere to any prescribed treatments. In fact, because of the psychologist's review of the tapes and a subsequent report suggesting schizophrenia, the prosecutors and I were actually optimistic that medical intervention could be the best long-term solution for everyone involved.

As the hearing approached, though, I began to wonder if the order was really necessary. I hadn't spotted the suspect on any more occasions, which made it easier for me to slip back into my everyday routine and minimize the fact that this armed stranger had spent hours focusing his rage at me. Sometimes friends would even try to jolt me back to vigilance by reminding me of the empty glass I'd found on the kitchen counter. "Unrelated," I told myself, so I could justify dismissing the case—and avoid the greater intrusion of ongoing criminal proceedings.

It finally took a patient district attorney to persuade me that a protective order could actually reestablish my personal boundaries. Once it was executed, if the suspect came within one hundred feet of me, he would be arrested on more serious charges.

Even though the hearing was supposed to be just a formality, the district attorney's office did suggest I bring along a lawyer for moral support. I was still struggling financially and approached Wesley, but he'd already used up his legal favors by trying to extricate Mark from drug-related charges in five different counties. So I was accompanied by the vice-president of Rogers State, who despite his background in criminal justice, was barred from the courtroom as soon as we arrived, an early indication that the afternoon would not proceed according to plan.

Once I was on the witness stand, the defense attorney, who'd been so gracious over the phone, apparently reneged on his deal with the prosecution and had me confirm that I'd expressed compassion for the suspect during our phone conversation. "Yes," I acknowledged, "but—" Never mind. My efforts to put the remarks in proper context, to distinguish *compassion* from *passion*, were cut off abruptly, and I was forced to respond to these complex, life-altering questions with simple "yes" or "no" answers. I was speechless by judicial decree and looked out into the gallery, desperate for a smile, eye contact, any indication of support. Only a young woman, taking notes, nodded her encouragement.

During further cross-examination, I also had to acknowledge an honest discrepancy between the facts and the official report. I had told the police department that I'd seen the suspect one morning at an intersection on my way to work, which had somehow been misunderstood to suggest that he'd been following me rather than waiting for me. Again, as I tried to make the clarification in court, I became suspect myself, and the judge wanted to know if I'd ever been *romantically* attracted to this man, this attic misfit who'd been so anonymous to me that I'd spent hours with the police puzzling over his identity.

As it turned out, several protective orders were issued that day, establishing boundaries between parents and wayward children, lovers and ex-lovers, even pet owners and post-men. But in my case, the gavel was less accommodating and resounded with the stalker-friendly decision, "petition denied," which meant the suspect had been temporarily vindicated, perhaps emboldened. The judge even inadvertently established a link between us—beyond this man's imagination. We were both going to be at the mercy of his mental illness.

The prosecution team rallied almost immediately and promised to renegotiate with the suspect's attorney to delay the stalking trial in exchange for an uncontested protective order. Apparently this had been the defense strategy all along and did result in my getting the official order within the next few days. I also received an unexpected boost from the young woman I'd spotted in the courtroom. A reporter for the local newspaper, she wrote a forceful editorial using my case to illustrate the legal conundrum for stalking and assault victims—if we sought legal remedies, we ended up being accused ourselves.

And not just within the court system. One Tahlequah police officer, when called upon to investigate a second pilfering incident at the house, advised me not to walk naked in front of the blinds, as if that were my modus operandi. Even friends and colleagues I'd known for years began asking me what I had done to provoke the man. Not that I blamed them. I tormented myself with the same question, wondering if I'd somehow given him encouragement without ever realizing it. After all, one of the sound bites on the last tape had been the Beatles' lyric, "I should have known better with a girl like you." Another favorite line from another favorite song made fearsome.

Oddly enough, the notion that I might somehow be responsible even provided me with a false sense of security, as if by altering my own behavior, I could take charge of the situation itself. But that just wasn't the reality, and fortunately John and other experienced investigators refused to let me delude myself with that kind of thinking. If the man phoned, they warned me, or tried to contact me in person, I would only put myself in more danger by trying to reason with him.

Because this man's actions were beyond the scope of ordinary wrongdoing, the kind I'd encountered at Flaming Rainbow and was capable of myself if placed in similar circumstances—without grocery or rent money. His veiled threats, the intrusions, weren't about someone's livelihood—*stalking* was about putting lives at stake in such a cavalier way that it seemed like gamesmanship.

∽

> Grandma Miller's attic wasn't a place where she stored holiday ornaments. She had downstairs closets for those items. Her attic, fully paneled in cedar, was the highpoint of her house, where she reflected on her favorite keepsakes, most notably her cup-and-saucer collection representing the fifty states. She and Grandpa had visited several of the states together, and she'd relied on relatives to pick up the other sets for her during their travels. Only two states weren't accounted for—Utah, because of her dispute with the governor, and Idaho. "Someone," she'd say, "has memories—secrets—in Idaho and has to steal to hold onto them."

∽

Shortly after the hearing, I began receiving hang-up calls at home and at work. We didn't have caller identification in the mid-1990s, so, just to be on the safe side—not for legal purposes—we assumed they were from the suspect. The psychologist had warned that the kind of intensity evidenced in the tapes didn't just suddenly dissipate, and John suggested the best strategy might be to change up my routine as much as possible.

Several friends had invited me to stay with them on a

rotating basis and would often receive hang-up calls themselves the mornings after my sleepovers. I didn't want to
place anyone else in jeopardy, but Lori, the first to open
up her home as a sanctuary, put it like this: countenancing
threatening behavior made everyone vulnerable. Lori and
her boys couldn't have been more vigilant on my behalf.
One morning, after hearing a car idling outside their house,
they all rushed out to confront the newspaper boy.

Another neighbor zeroed in on a man doing some yard
work for me while I was at school. The man, who'd served
some time for a nonviolent offense, was so discomfited
when the police arrived that, as much as he needed the job,
he decided to look for work in a "safer" part of town.

So the trick for us, most especially me, was to keep an eye
out for the stalker without seeing him everywhere.

I also had to be careful not to let him define me or my
relationships. Other friends were understandably uneasy
about being associated with me during such an unsettling
time and didn't feel they could be seen with me at mov-
ies or in restaurants without placing themselves and their
families in jeopardy. Even Wesley was convinced that the
stalker had targeted him by rifling through his garage. But I
couldn't—despite any initial hurt—suddenly discount these
people and the contributions they'd made to my life based
on these new circumstances. We were all being tested in different ways, and I was grateful for whatever token support
they could provide—gifts of pepper spray, books on self-
defense, even bullets for the gun I didn't own.

I was still spending some nights at home, just not on a
regular basis. I'd had a security system installed, but I was
too uneasy to let myself be distracted by any noise of my
own making. Instead of watching television, I read and
reread Carson McCullers's *The Member of the Wedding*
and liked to imagine myself inside the sweltering Geor-
gia kitchen that John Henry, Berenice, and the motherless

Frankie had consecrated with their makeshift family. *Sweltering*, for me, even more than Frankie's mother-loss, was the link between us as we moved into spring and I couldn't bear the clanking/perceived risk of my old window air-conditioner. I made a deal with Skylar to turn it on for ten minutes every hour, and we'd kneel before the old Fedders as if it were an altar.

And in a way it was, because we were making all sorts of sacrifices—at least with respect to physical and mental comfort. Whenever we stayed at homes with central air, I could see the toll our new lifestyle was taking on Skylar. The big orange tabby would forgo food to spend his time spread-eagled over the floor vents, savoring the rush of cold air through his fur and purring incessantly.

One of my cousins had called to suggest I relocate to Oklahoma City, where I could become more anonymous, and John told me that some women in similar situations actually did move to different towns—and in some cases changed their identities—so they could avoid the stress of waiting for something worse to happen. Of course no one could say for sure that this man would continue to be more aggressive, and we were still pursuing the criminal charges. But all of the law-enforcement officials who'd visited his attic concurred—their instincts told them that a man who'd surrounded himself with all the trappings of violence wasn't going to stop until he'd fulfilled his own fierce ambitions.

But, for me, moving was out of the question. I'd finally found a job I enjoyed, and without it I didn't have the means to relocate for any reason, though I still entertained notions of living in New York one day and realizing my writer dreams in an artistic community like SoHo. In the meantime, I was surprised and delighted to be discovering an extensive and accessible network of Oklahoma writers through my outreach at Rogers State.

Soon after settling into my teaching post, I'd been offered a fifteen-minute segment on the school radio station to showcase my writing students. We called the program *Writing Out Loud* and produced an ongoing melodrama, "In Search of Miss Fortune," about a missing heiress. The program became so popular within the community that we continued it the next year with "The Return of Miss Fortune." I emceed the show, and in the process of assuming a microphone on live radio and of regularly standing in front of classrooms packed with students—who always noticed the runners in my stockings—I began to overcome my fear of public speaking. I was on a tight budget emotionally as well as financially, and I just couldn't indulge myself anymore.

By the time the college offered me my own television version of *Writing Out Loud*, which was to feature half-hour, taped interviews with established writers, my accent had even become my trademark. It's important to note that I had no training in television whatsoever, and this wasn't just to be a Claremore show. The college station covered a large section of northeastern Oklahoma, and so I'd be learning broadcasting in front of a substantial, though forgiving audience.

As host-producer, I was responsible for lining up guests and suddenly started to appreciate Oklahoma's unique literary heritage. John's admonition that I needed to be aware of my surroundings was beginning to take on extended meaning—I needed to be aware of them in a positive sense as well, and I was amazed to find so many fine, even famous writers living within driving distance.

One of my first interviews featured *Route 66* author Michael Wallis, who'd adopted Oklahoma as his home. His commanding voice and unabashed love for the state put Steinbeck in perspective for me once and for all. I also visited with mystery novelists Jean Hager and Carolyn G. Hart, who were so prolific—no writer's block for them—that they couldn't even keep track of how many books they'd written. And I was especially intrigued by true-crime writer Darcy O'Brien, whose haunting work about the Hillside Stranglers was offset by the artistry of his literary commentary on the conscience of James Joyce, an important reminder to counterbalance violence with art in my own life.

Since I was so eager for literary company and had so many questions to ask, most of these interviews came easily to me. The only early guest who filled me with nervous anticipation was S. E. Hinton, the legendary author of *The Outsiders*, who was known to be reclusive. I'd contacted her through a mutual friend and was astounded when she agreed to be on the program. Fans of Hinton's work are familiar with her incredible story, how she wrote *The Outsiders* when she was only sixteen, creating the genre of young-adult literature. Then she quickly followed that success with a series of other groundbreaking novels and movie collaborations with such directors as Francis Ford Coppola and actors as Matt Dillon.

Of course it was hard not to make comparisons. Hinton and I were about the same age, and I was intimidated by her celebrity, especially upon meeting her for the first time in our basement studio. Even shaking hands with her was a little awkward for me because I literally had to come to grips with someone who'd shared a similar dream and gone farther with it. I asked what I should call her.

"Either Susie or Your Majesty," she said in such an unassuming way that when I settled on Susie—without pretense—I was more at ease with her and myself.

∽

Wesley, who'd been stationed in Hawaii during World War II, returned to the islands after my stepmother's death, supposedly to enjoy their tropical beauty, but he finally confessed to my cousin that he'd gone searching

for a lost love, a woman of color he'd hoped to marry
long before he'd met my mother. Apparently Grandma
Miller had opposed the union with such vehemence
that he'd forsaken the relationship without ever letting
it go. His subsequent trips to locate this lover always
failed, and he returned to Tahlequah with too many
brightly colored shirts. After a while, he started his own
collection—Hawaiian postcards—generic pictures of all
that was left to him. Sometimes, even before my prob-
lems, he got hang-up calls, probably wrong numbers,
but he'd keep the receiver pressed to his ear until the
dial tone returned, ending any speculation.

~

In the spring of 1994 Mark was found guilty of drug trafficking and sentenced to four years in prison. Wesley and
I hadn't attended the trial. We'd become estranged from
Mark, but not in the sense that we were feuding. Instead,
we'd literally become *strangers* to him and felt our presence
would only make his ordeal more difficult. Our other concern had been that we might be called to testify against him,
and we'd both known beyond a reasonable doubt, beyond
any doubt, that he was guilty—we just couldn't figure out
why he'd gone from using drugs for his own purposes to
becoming a dealer and manufacturer.

The easy explanation was that he'd been desperate to
finance his own habit, but he'd only been a bush-league
trafficker and could have made more money by practicing
the law than breaking it. That's why our cousin, who was
defending him, had already forewarned us that the court
wouldn't be sympathetic, for as a young, engaging attorney,
Mark personified privilege—or so it seemed.

According to our cousin, Mark had broken only once
during the course of the trial, when he'd asked for leni-
ency to be with his son, for despite his shortcomings he'd
remained devoted to Jonathan in a way no one had ever
been devoted to Mark himself. Material privilege can be

so misleading. In some ways Mark, who'd never known a mother's love, had grown up with *less* than most people.

Wesley had called me on my cell phone with news of the verdict as I was driving home from work, and at first we both assailed each other with random talk and speculation. I'd suddenly remembered what Grandma had told me, that the family had left Mark in the hospital longer than usual because of the shock of Mother's death, and I wondered what role that might have played. And Wesley kept noting how Mark had been so blatant in his transgressions, even when he'd known he was under surveillance, that perhaps he'd wanted to get caught. But we stopped ourselves. The decision had been made. What more could we say? Even so, we couldn't quite let go of our connection, despite the static. We left the phone line open for the rest of my commute without saying another word.

Ironically, Mark and I were both being highlighted in area newspapers that spring—for Mark's conviction and my stalking case. Wesley noted that he'd always wanted his children to be recognized outside Tahlequah, just not in these ways. Already he worried that the stalking incident, which he didn't take seriously, would overshadow what I'd accomplished with the novel and the television show.

The stalking case kept getting scheduled and rescheduled, and we had a new court date set for later that spring. Since the initial hearing for the protective order had been so traumatic, I'd become increasingly reluctant to pursue the charges, choosing instead to focus on as many happy diversions as possible. I asked what would happen if I refused to show for the trial and was told a bench warrant could be issued for *my* arrest. But this wasn't a threat—John and the prosecutors explained that if we were diligent, we would have a rare opportunity to stop a crime before it happened, that other lives might be at stake as well.

The entire Claremore police force continued to be more

than cautious with my well-being. At times of heightened risk, when they felt the suspect might be inclined to retaliate because of pending court actions, they'd wait for me in the parking lot after my night class, then follow me to a friend's home in town. The general consensus all along had been that I was most vulnerable on the road, so at least when I was within the jurisdiction of Rogers County, I was under the protective watch of law enforcement.

Though I couldn't help being anxious when I was in the car, I tried not to let perceived threats curtail my travels any more than necessary. True, I found myself checking the rearview mirror relentlessly, and I always kept my phone by my side, but I still enjoyed my time behind the wheel, particularly when I got the opportunity to make provocative side trips.

One afternoon my professor friend in Tahlequah asked me to swing by the Tulsa airport to pick up author Joyce Carol Thomas. Joyce, a National Book Award winner, was scheduled to appear at Northeastern, so I would have a passenger, a writer even, to take me in a new direction and accompany me the rest of the way home. I'd long been an admirer of Joyce's work and was so excited about the prospect of visiting with her that I ran my purse through airport security with such detachment that I looked to everyone else when the security lights began flashing.

But the officers, three of them, weren't approaching one of the other airport visitors; they were after me, actually closing ranks around me and ushering me into a back room. Why, they wanted to know, did I have bullets in my purse? *The bullets.* I'd forgotten all about them—one of those gifts from people who weren't quite sure how to demonstrate their support. In fairness to them, Hallmark doesn't have occasional cards for these kinds of life transitions. Of course I knew in advance from the tough looks I was getting that the classic line, "A friend gave them to me," wasn't going to extricate me. Luckily I had the protective order in my purse, and, after reviewing it and questioning me thoroughly, the officers released me to meet Joyce.

Joyce's plane had already arrived, but I found her in the front lobby and introduced myself by explaining I'd been detained by airport security. When she asked for more details, I told her that I'd had bullets in my purse and briefly filled her in on the stalker situation.

"Bullets," she repeated, her eyes locking with mine. Since I was her designated driver, the person charged with her safety, she had to make a quick choice: trust me completely or not at all. She decided to trust me, and that telling moment defined our relationship. We were close friends, sisters in spirit, by the time we got to Tahlequah.

❧

Mark, assigned to a prison several miles from us, immediately wrote Jonathan a letter from his cell. He did not address his living conditions, at least not in a conventional way. Without giving Jonathan any sense of how challenging his circumstances were, he wrote with great eloquence about his devotion to him and how they would emerge from this time, this incarceration, with renewed strength. So what could have been a cold, even heartless room, of the imagination in my mind at least, has been transformed in such a way that it bears a bronze plaque—similar to the ones I saw in Virginia— declaring simply: Jonathan's Father Slept Here.

❧

I didn't go to the stalker's arraignment, but my friends Art and Genell Dellin went on my behalf so they could get a sense of the man and advise me. Their report wasn't encouraging. Genell, a gifted novelist, was especially astute at judging character, and she found the man's frenzied demeanor unsettling. I was getting similar opinions from officers and others who'd had direct dealings with him. If anything, his condition was deteriorating and for some reason his mother wasn't—at least from what we could tell—encouraging him to accept our offer to drop the charges if he would agree to psychiatric treatment.

All this is to say that I came to a decision that was so contrary to any of my previous beliefs that it still startles me, a liberal Democrat, after all these years. I went to a firearms store one day after work, bought a gun, and enrolled in a gun-safety course with Art and Genell. The determining factor for me had been the psychologist's growing belief that if this man, armed himself, ever did get the drop on me, he would be very vindictive. And though I was taking every reasonable precaution, when I was alone on the road—or even at home—I had no real way to defend myself. The very fact that I'd kept those bullets in my purse told me that I'd actually been harboring this idea all along as a last resort.

Once I started the course itself, I had to make another hard decision. The instructor told us that we shouldn't have a gun at all unless we were prepared to use it, and that possibility became more real to us when we actually fired our weapons at human outlines on the shooting range. My first attempts weren't even close, and I continued to miss the target on subsequent trials that evening. Afterwards, my overall scores were so low I had to seriously reexamine my intentions. Did I truly have it in me to defend my life by taking another?

Years before—as part of my first stepmother's abusive behavior, which was still a taboo subject—she'd dropped me into a construction pit in our city park. My life hadn't truly been in jeopardy, but, only five at the time, I'd been terrified at first, huddling in the damp darkness and crying for grandmothers who couldn't hear me. After a while, I'd had a choice to make—stay in the pit and wait for help (if it came) or rescue myself and climb out on my own. It took me several tries, but finally I made it to level ground and realized the pit hadn't been so deep after all. Still I'd learned something important about myself—I was a survivor.

It was as a survivor that I came to the conclusion that, yes, I could shoot to save my life, as distasteful as the prospect might be, but such wrenching self-knowledge was sobering for me. Even though I remained a firm believer in gun control, I'd find myself on the defensive, even when it wasn't necessary. One day, when I was in the checkout line at Wal-Mart paying for a tube of lipstick, the cashier asked, "Do you want that in your purse?"

Of course, she meant the lipstick, but I was so self-conscious about carrying a gun, that I replied, "No, but I feel like my life depends on it." I don't mean to pass this off as an amusing anecdote. It is a serious example of how fear can work its way into our everyday routines and force us to come to terms with who we are. As it turned out, three of my women colleagues at Rogers State, afraid that the stalker might threaten us in our workplace, had also come to this understanding in their own lives.

∾

When I was in high school, Wesley took me to a small Native American school in Twin Oaks, Oklahoma, to meet Robert Kennedy, who, in his capacity as senator, was doing on-site visits to assess the state of Indian education in our country. The school was a modest structure, with graffiti-covered desks and linoleum floors, but as Kennedy stood before its dusty blackboards, he was asking its students and their teachers to join him on the world's stage. A few months later he was assassinated in Los Angeles, and the bullets ricocheted all the way back to Twin Oaks, where he was mourned as a brother—and fellow student.

∾

Later that summer Jonathan came to spend the weekend with me, but we didn't talk about prison or the stalker.

Despite the fact that I'd been frustrated as a child because the family wouldn't openly address our problems, I was repeating that same mistake with Jonny. In fact I was overcompensating to such an extent that our time together felt more like a visit to an amusement park than a relaxed weekend. I'd overstocked on videos, ice cream, and a new computer game—for myself as much as him.

We'd exhausted ourselves within a few hours, and Jonny suggested we might just watch a little quiet TV, maybe even channel surf, but regular programming had been preempted by the infamous O. J. Bronco chase, so I quickly set up another computer session with *Where in the World Is Carmen San Diego?* I was still chasing Carmen around Paris, when I glanced over my shoulder and saw that Jonathan had fallen asleep reading *Danger on the Homestead,* a book by Oklahoma author Bessie Holland Heck. Apparently he had discovered his own means of transit.

As I watched him, resting so peacefully in the midst of our family turmoil, I had a telling flashback. One weekend six years before, we'd stood in front of the house admiring marching bands, floats, and rodeo horses aligning themselves for a parade that would wind its way down Main Street. Only six at the time, he'd been especially intrigued by the restless horses and had slipped from my grasp to tug at their reins and claim their energy as his own.

Finally, I'd pulled him aside, explained the risks, and emphasized that, as hard as it was for him to understand, I just wanted him to be safe and happy. That's when he'd looked up at me, tears streaming down his cheeks, and pleaded, "Please, please, don't make me be happy." I could hear him so clearly—through all the years—all the sorrows—that I picked out a book of my own, Anne Tyler's *The Accidental Tourist,* and joined him on the couch, where he'd subtly redirected the tempo of our entire weekend.

We were so at ease with each other by Sunday that we

took back the rest of our videos and went crawdad fishing in the town branch on the university campus. Though we didn't catch many crawdads by overloading our strings with bacon and dangling them along the banks, we enjoyed competing in a sport that didn't penalize losers. Any crawdads we did happen to snag, Jonny immediately released back into the current.

I couldn't help but respect the way Jonny took so much pleasure in returning them to their natural habitat, stretching himself to the limit to drop them as far out of harm's way as possible. At one point a man on a bike pedaled past us and exchanged a nod of recognition, which I assumed registered our joint admiration for Jonny. Jonny was a fine-looking boy with Mark's/Grandma's large blue eyes, strikingly offset by his discerning dark brows, a gentle smile, and, of course, that crawdad-friendly demeanor.

But the respite with Jonny was short-lived. The telephone started ringing just a few minutes after his mother picked him up to return to their home in Kansas, Oklahoma. This time, though, instead of just settling for abrupt, click-down-the-receiver threats, the caller was breathing heavily and suggestively, or at least that was the case when I answered the first few times. I finally decided to ignore whoever it was, and the calls eventually stopped after another hour or so.

Jonny and I had spent such a nice weekend together that I had to work at getting scared, but after it was dark, I reminded myself to be guarded and started listening for trouble above the clamor of the Joan Rivers biopic I was watching on local television. Joan Rivers and her daughter were playing themselves, which was just tasteless enough to keep my fears in perspective. Later as I stared at the phone and thought back over all the tapes and court appearances, so unbelievable, I began to feel as if I were playing myself, too.

I'd already warned Skylar that we wouldn't be getting any air-conditioner breaks that night, but even though it was hot, I went to bed in my jeans and slept fitfully. Perhaps it was the nature of the calls themselves that left me so uneasy—or maybe it was the cumulative effect of all our family troubles finally coalescing after so many years of denial. Whatever the reason, I was filled with a sense of foreboding that was ultimately realized shortly after midnight, when I was awakened by a heavy thud, followed almost immediately by the blare of my security alarm.

The instructor in our gun-safety class had told us that we should never try to make a run for it, that we should hold our positions—weapons engaged—in a dark room and wait for help to arrive. But I panicked. I could see that the front door hadn't been breached, so after failing to locate Skylar, I bolted, escaping into the street and literally bumping into the couple from next door just as they returned from an Indian powwow. Ron, a former Vietnam vet turned Indian medicine man, checked the perimeters of the yard, and everything seemed secure. The police also arrived and gave the all-clear for the inside of the house, too. One of the officers phoned the security company and learned that the front door had set off the alarm, probably when the intruder had lunged into the door itself, trying to dislodge it from the doorjamb. So if I hadn't been lucky enough to meet up with Ron, my hasty response could have brought me face-to-face with the culprit.

Ron's wife had called Lori, and she'd come to take me to her house for the night, but not before we tracked down Skylar, hiding under the bed, claws poised for attack. His instincts had been more reliable than mine, though he was none too happy about being trapped in a house with a blaring siren for over a half hour. Ever since, he's been a firm believer in preemptive strikes, and now he's listed at the vet's as a Republican and "known biter."

Before Lori and I packed for her house, we visited with some of the neighbors from across the street, most of them misfits themselves, who'd rented apartments in what had once been a beautifully maintained, upscale boarding house for professors and their students. One of the new occupants, a middle-aged woman, told me she'd seen a man lurking on the street, who—she admitted this would seem odd—was riding a bicycle erratically. When we asked her to describe him, she couldn't tell us much beyond dark hair and eyes.

Already I'd made the connection with the bicyclist who'd exchanged glances with me earlier in the day, when Jonny and I had been crawdad fishing. Could he have been the stalker? I'd been so preoccupied with Jonny that I hadn't paid much attention to the man himself. Besides, it had never occurred to me to look for the stalker during a casual outing with my nephew in the heart of our hometown.

But, yes, I told John the next morning, the man did bear a resemblance to the pictures he'd given me of the suspect, though I couldn't in good conscience make a positive identification. So we would have to continue speculating: Was just one man involved in all these incidents? Or were we living in a world gone so awry that we had other predators among us, striking at random? I didn't even know how to direct my hopes; either prospect was terrifying.

～

One day my older friend Dorothy phoned to tell me she was ill, and I promised to call her later to see how she was doing. When I did, I barely recognized her voice and was shocked by how much she'd deteriorated. Then I realized that I'd dialed the wrong number, the wrong Dorothy, and apologized profusely. Imagine the odds. "But I'm still sick," this Dorothy told me, because even though we were strangers, we shared a 918 area code. The connection was tenuous, but we lived within

the same margin of error, that uncharted territory of
chance encounters—consecrated with our clumsiness.

∾

The next Saturday afternoon, after returning home from the grocery store, I had a voice message waiting for me. Obviously the caller was trying to disguise his voice, but his recording was clear: "I saw you out on the street last week and will be back to see you tonight."

I asked the Tahlequah police to come over, and they listened to the tape without drawing any definitive conclusions. They did, however, warn me to be even more alert than usual. A few hours later, Lori and I were both in separate cars, coming from opposite directions, when we spotted a bicyclist that we believed to be the stalker. The fact that we'd identified him independently convinced us even more, but after the police tracked him down, they dismissed him as a stalker look-alike. We even wondered ourselves if we weren't "imagining things," Wesley's contention and something we had to consider during such stressful times.

Lori and her son had already invited me to dinner on the lake, and they picked me up later that afternoon. Even though we were tense, we enjoyed a leisurely meal, and it was after dark when we returned to find a crowd gathered at the house. My car, parked out front, had been smashed on the driver's side, and the only witnesses, some little children from across the street, said a truck had deliberately backed into the car—twice.

Of course they'd been too young and startled to get a clear description of the truck or a tag number; they couldn't even remember for sure what color the truck was. My initial hope was that we could check out the suspect's vehicles for trace evidence and run a voice analysis of the answering-machine tape. But even John explained that wouldn't be feasible. In addition to being cost-prohibitive, an extended investigation would bring up jurisdictional issues. This was a Tahlequah crime and, unless the Oklahoma Bureau of Investigation became involved, we wouldn't be able to initiate investigations across county lines.

My situation—being threatened without the advantage of established safeguards—prompted many of my friends, who felt uneasy themselves, to propose desperate measures that were terrifying in and of themselves. A well-known author I'd interviewed on *Writing Out Loud* had experienced problems with stalkers over the years and offered to have his bodyguard break the kneecaps of the man who'd been harassing me. Still another acquaintance, who worked at a local car dealership, pulled me aside at a community gathering to say that, as a Vietnam vet, he'd already had to kill and that he would like to murder the man for me—for all of us.

Even a retired police officer suggested that I secretly entice the suspect to my house, shoot him, and avoid prosecution by claiming my rights under the "Make My Day Law," which allowed Oklahomans to kill intruders who broke into their homes.

Other friends and associates advocated nonviolent alternatives that were also controversial. My neighbor Ron was prepared to bring down "bad medicine" on the suspect. A very spiritual man, Ron promised he would invoke the dark forces only if we ran out of other options. In the meantime, he was a kindhearted vigilante. He knew how determined I was to keep up regular visits with Jonny—all I could do for Mark—but that I worried about the boy's safety. During one of Jonny's sleepovers, Ron assured me he'd be watching our house from his. And sure enough, whenever I'd pull back the curtains that evening, I'd find Ron's stalwart shadow in the light of his picture window.

Yet despite Ron's kindness, Grandma's neighborhood

just wasn't the same anymore, and I couldn't expect it to be the safe haven it had been for me as a child. So I sold my legacy—at least that's how it felt—to move to a more secure part of town. I couldn't blame the stalker alone for uprooting me. The neighborhood had been impacted by urban renewal and had shifted its focus from established homes to transient housing. Even Ron planned to move within a few months, so I wasn't really located at 117 W. Morgan; I was lost there, trying to keep my bearings straight by relying on old landmarks.

Though I looked forward to moving to a new home, here I was surrounded by neighbors I'd known my entire life, and I understood I couldn't pack everything. Grandma had designed her house in the early 1950s, while Mother and Wesley had been building a place, too. They'd used the same contractor and had developed even deeper bonds as they'd made joint decisions about countertops and color schemes. It was that fleeting sense of family normalcy—hidden beneath layers of paint—that I would miss the most. For even Grandma had anticipated harder times ahead when she'd mounted the light switches lower than usual, so her grandchildren could reach them in the dark. She'd also rounded the corners in the hallway so we could run at top speed without the threat of any sharp obstacles—at least for a few years.

Since her death, I'd tried to make the house my own by taking liberties that would have shocked her. I'd fallen in love in the living room, watching *Tender Mercies* with a man I hadn't married. I'd learned to mix scotch with water in the kitchen, though occasionally I preferred it straight. I'd gotten a cat for the backyard, but Skylar had since moved into my bedroom, where we kept the gun. And I'd painted the outside of the house blue. When I asked Lori once which of these infractions would have troubled Grandma most, she didn't have to think about it—the cat.

But as I was doing a final walk-through of the house, collecting the few reminders I'd carry with me, I suddenly felt the kind of chill I usually experienced while visiting a famous mansion like the Hermitage or a great battlefield like Gettysburg. For I'd distanced myself just enough to recognize this home for what it truly was, not the "fixer-upper" the realtor had advertised, but the place where Grandma and Grandpa had overcome the loss of their only daughter—where they'd managed, despite their hurt, to foster hope in their grandchildren—and where they'd ultimately lived out their own final days with dignity. I was on sacred ground.

∾

When I was in grade school, our teachers arranged for us to tour the Murrell Home, a Cherokee mansion that had survived the Civil War. The curator, who'd rarely had so many visitors, was overly anxious to impress restless children and tried to get our attention by listing all the important personages who'd been guests of the Murrells. Later, I told Grandma that I'd walked in the steps of Abraham Lincoln that day, but she broke the news that the curator had storied to us. She took me back herself, showed me the slave quarters, and subsequently rebuilt the mansion for me with names I'd never heard before but still remember.

∾

Because of the success of the television show, Rogers State gave me opportunity to start my own literary center, the Oklahoma Center for Poets and Writers, which would continue producing *Writing Out Loud* and also sponsor an annual Celebration of Books, a conference that would bring writers and readers together in a festive atmosphere. I was especially intrigued by the idea of the Celebration, because I would be relying on a community of writers who, I hoped, would inspire not only others but also me.

Even though I was too preoccupied to write during the stalking ordeal, I knew that I had more stories to tell. Visiting with successful authors validated that dream, for they often shared the benefit of their experience. Novelist Nancy Pickard read an early draft of my novel-in-progress and gave me wonderful advice about switching from first to third person. She also showed me the professional courtesy of bluntness by asking, "Teresa, what are you going to do with yourself?" Years later she and psychologist Lynn Lott included a reference to my writer's block in their book, *Seven Steps on the Writer's Path.*

But writing dreams aside, I had another important reason for wanting to do the book festival—it was a welcome diversion from all the ongoing legal maneuvers in the stalking case. Discussions would sometimes subside for weeks at a time before suddenly coming to life again and resulting in a new schedule of court dates. A district attorney in an adjacent county was also pursuing drug charges, and whenever hearings were imminent in any of the various venues, I tended to receive more hang-up calls at work. The stalker had also threatened me indirectly by trying to visit Mark in prison. Mark, of course, had refused to see him. Despite his differences with Wesley and me, he wasn't about to condone this kind of menacing behavior toward his family—or anyone else for that matter.

So the subterfuge continued, and I needed to remind myself to be cautious as I began to focus almost exclusively on the festival. Since this would be our first big event, we needed a headliner, and I wrote a letter to novelist and PBS news anchor Jim Lehrer asking him to accept one of our awards. The catch was that we didn't have much to offer besides our undying gratitude, only a small honorarium and plane fare. Even as I sealed the envelope, I felt a rush of embarrassment, because I was a huge admirer of Jim's and didn't want him to think that our limited resources some-how lessened our appreciation of him.

Much to everyone's surprise, Jim wrote back almost immediately that he had *indeed* heard of Claremore and would accept our invitation on one condition—he didn't want to stay at the Elm Motel. The son of a Kansas bus driver, he'd traveled the circuit as a boy and knew which motels to avoid. But he needn't have worried about the Elm. Once word spread about his visit, we were inundated with invitations for him to stay in private homes. Some would-be hosts even became so competitive that they started un-dermining each other. If we'd been more enterprising, we could have launched a bidding war.

Fights also broke out over who would get to pick Jim up at the airport, but I'd chosen my friends Penny and Judy, knowing they would greet him with the proper decorum. In fact, they were so determined to make a good impression that they were in the restroom putting on lipstick when his plane arrived. Underpaid and seemingly abandoned, Jim had already placed an SOS call to Washington by the time they finally located him in front of the baggage carousels, but no apologies were necessary. The father of three daugh-ters, he understood the importance of lipstick.

That evening he opened his keynote address by doing a litany of bus route calls, prompting the audience to burst into applause when he used all of his skills as a former sta-tion agent to make "Claremore" resonate throughout the auditorium. He then turned his attention to a no-nonsense talk about the craft of writing, and I began to squirm back-stage when he emphasized the importance of discipline. But he was so matter-of-fact that later, when he extended his hand in friendship, I knew it wasn't an idle gesture.

We all experienced his warmth in a variety of ways, getting our photos taken with him, having our books personally inscribed. Though he'd interviewed virtually all of the world's leading political figures, we referred to him simply as Jim. After all, he was a guest in our homes five nights a week, and if there was bad news, he was the one who broke it to us and the one we counted on to keep it in perspective.

He had also become our trusted intermediary, brokering conversations between us and the people we wanted to know. One woman, who'd always been overly health conscious, told me that after meeting Jim, she didn't believe that "Six Degrees of Separation" still applied to her. She'd been just a sneeze or two away from President Clinton, the Pope, Princess Di, and . . . Her roster of famous names began to sound like one of Jim's station calls. But as he continued to engage with the crowd, it was clear that he hadn't made celebrity a priority in his own life. I just hoped to swap bus stories with him someday.

We were also featuring thirty other outstanding authors over the weekend, and I stayed with Judy so I could feel safe in the midst of so much goodwill, which we worried might conversely attract the stalker. But he was a no-show as far as we could tell, and just one crime was committed during the entire festival. Of all the hundreds of books that had been on sale for writers to autograph, only a single title had been stolen, *Think on These Things,* by religious essayist and inspirational columnist Joyce Hifler.

∽

In 1990 a Tulsa radio station spearheaded the drive to erect a monument honoring Mr. Ed the Talking Horse at his gravesite outside Tahlequah. The 1,000-pound granite replica of the horse had been the subject of my Tahlequah stories for years before one of my students, Maria DeLong, decided to write an article about the memorial. She made an unsettling discovery: the real Mr. Ed, aka Bamboo Harvester, had been cremated in

California. The Tahlequah horse, a rear-end double for
Ed in publicity stills, hadn't been nearly so well-spoken
and was only being immortalized thanks to six degrees
of fabrication.

∾

The book festival went so well that we decided to host a
follow-up event for area high school students that spring,
featuring Joyce Carol Thomas. I was en route to the Tulsa
airport to pick up Joyce on April 19, 1995, when I heard the
radio bulletin—the Alfred P. Murrah Federal Building in
Oklahoma City had been bombed. Details were still sketchy,
but even preliminary reports hinted at the bad news that
would follow: several federal workers and their children
had been killed; hundreds of others had been injured.

I could feel the aftershocks as I entered the airport,
where security officers were strategically positioned at
every entrance. Since rescue teams were being flown to
Oklahoma from around the country, all incoming flights,
including Joyce's, had been delayed. During the wait, I
thought about seeking out some of my extended family in
Tulsa, but instead I joined the airport vigil, not a formal
ceremony of any kind, but a gathering of restless travelers
and expectant friends, all of us painfully reminded of the
transience of life and looking to the television monitors for
reassurances.

Joyce didn't arrive until after dark, and as she and the
other passengers entered the terminal, they seemed to
stoop beneath the added weight of their journey. Later, as
we headed toward Claremore, Joyce explained that relief
workers and cadaver dogs had been on the plane with them
as far as Oklahoma City. She had gotten to know many of
the workers and their dogs personally during the flight and
spoke of them with such great affection that I knew a part
of her was in Oklahoma City, too.

The night itself was volatile, and we were under a tornado

watch. As we drove through heavy showers, we talked for a while about whether we should even proceed with the planned program the next day, but Joyce persuaded me that it was more important than ever for us to join together, not for the celebration we'd anticipated, but for the consolation we needed. Oklahoma was accustomed to nature's wrath, and we'd all rallied in the past to overcome devastating storms, but to be targeted by other human beings, perhaps fellow Oklahomans, was an incomprehensible sadness.

I'd already decided to rent a motel room in Claremore next to Joyce's, so she wouldn't be alone in town under the circumstances and so I wouldn't have to drive even farther in the threatening weather. Ever since I'd bought the new house in Tahlequah, friends had been telling me that I should have moved to Claremore instead and spared myself the commute. But most nights Tahlequah, with its familiar storefronts, was a refuge for me; this night, Joyce was.

As much as I enjoyed Joyce's talents as a writer, I was equally in awe of her ability to rechannel negative experiences in a way that enriched all those around her. Though she'd encountered racism while growing up in Oklahoma, she continued to love the state for what it could be. She'd even transformed the racial slur—"The Gold Dust Twins," a take-off from a brand-name scouring powder—into a term of endearment. Her poem by that title, about her special relationship with her sister, had touched so many readers, including me, that we longed for that same distinction in our own lives. So if anyone could settle our uneasy spirits in the aftermath of the bombing, Joyce was that person.

The flags were already flying at half-mast when we arrived at the college early the next morning to greet startled high-school students and their teachers. Joyce understood her new role and selected poems such as "Cherish Me" that eased us through the hours by addressing our grief and celebrating our common humanity. The campus clock, a novelty, always chimed the tune to "Oh, what a beautiful mornin', / Oh, what a beautiful day" from the musical *Oklahoma*, but on this not-so-beautiful day, the hourly refrain was an uneasy reminder of all that had transpired during the last twenty-four-hour cycle.

Though I'd been heartened by the healing time with Joyce, the drive to Tahlequah that evening seemed longer and darker than usual, and I was relieved to get back home. Skylar purred reassuringly as he joined me in the garage to help me unpack, and I was already anticipating a quiet weekend. I'd just stepped inside with my suitcase when he began screeching. He'd jumped on top of the car trunk, closing the lid on his leg, and was so frantic that he bit me repeatedly as I struggled to free him. We were both bleeding profusely by the time I made it to the phone.

Lori, now my new neighbor, took me to the emergency room, where we spent several hours talking about the bombing while we waited for the doctor. Lori's brother, Phil, a judicial officer, had been in the building across the street from the Murrah Building. Though he hadn't been injured, he'd worked tirelessly to free victims from the debris and, like so many, was wounded emotionally. Phil's close call seemed to have made Lori more aware of the danger potential for all of us. Before we'd left for the hospital, she'd insisted we take the extra time to bolt all the doors, and when we got back, well after midnight, she came into the house with me and made sure all was safe before I activated the alarm system.

But I felt so emboldened just being at home—Skylar returned the next afternoon from the vet's sporting a cast— that when I answered the phone that Saturday, I wasn't the least bit apprehensive. I looked forward to visiting with any friend who might be calling to check on us. Except this colleague from Claremore had startling news: according to her relatives in the sheriff's department, the stalker had been arrested late the previous night for murdering his mother.

"His mother," I repeated, for even though I was stunned, the irony didn't escape me. I would have forgiven my own mother any transgression to have her with me again and couldn't begin to fathom the kinds of opposing forces that had somehow placed this man and me together in the same frightening sphere.

A few minutes later, John called with more of the details. Apparently, the stalker had beaten his mother to death with a claw hammer the night of the bombing and had been hiding her body in the house ever since. No one knew where he had been spending his time the last couple of days, but the mother's brother and nephew had found him in his truck, getting ready to leave.

Initially the family had become suspicious when the mother hadn't responded to their repeated messages about an aunt's death. The stalker had been insisting she was at work, but they'd checked with the hospital where she was a nurse, only to learn that she hadn't been reporting for her regular shifts. It wasn't until he was arrested that the stalker, now a murderer, told authorities that he'd believed she was giving him poisonous shots. But as one investigator put it, "There is no logical explanation." In addition to brutalizing the woman, he'd also doused her body in gasoline and wired it to an electric coffeepot, so it appeared his plans had included setting a fire, too.

As I sorted through all the grisly details, I kept coming back to the fact that no one had known where the stalker had been for the past couple of nights, while I'd been *away* with Joyce in Claremore and *away* with Lori in the emergency room.

Then John said it: "This could have happened to you."

∽

After Kate Smullen died, her cabin became a restaurant until the lease expired, and the eatery, still called Echota or "contentment," began operating out of a modern home across town. Once I took Joyce to dinner there and noticed a woman staring at her from another table. I worried at first that the woman might be recalling past prejudices and looking to Joyce, the only other African American in the room. But then she approached us and ventured, "Joyce?" A friend of Joyce's from California, she was visiting her daughter, who'd just moved to Tahlequah. Of course, we were struck by the serendipity, but even more so by the fact that the franchised goodwill of Echota could be so far-reaching.

⁓

By the next weekend, I was able to fully enjoy a beautiful spring day again. I'd even left the front door standing open, so I could let the scent of honeysuckle overcome any stale apprehension that still lingered in the house. But I didn't get to indulge myself long before a Tahlequah police officer was standing on the porch, warning me about the door. "You must not have heard," I told him. "It's over. He's been arrested and will probably spend the rest of his life in prison." The officer knew, though, and was there to tell me the rest of the story—it still wasn't safe to be so trusting, even in Tahlequah.

A few nights later, I had a nightmare. As required by law, I'd stopped behind a school bus, and the stalker had jumped out with a group of children to confront me: "You never thought I'd be driving a school bus, did you?" It wasn't a complicated dream to analyze. I'd been tricked by my own innocence.

We'd never know for sure how many of the frightening incidents in my life were directly linked to the stalker. The attempted break-in at my house, for instance, could have been a coincidence. In fact, looking anxiously over my shoulder for the past two years had made me even more aware of lives intersecting in unexpected ways. Some synchronicity could be quirky, harmless—a man I once loved married a woman who once loved Mark, and they had our mother's harmonica. I liked to tell that story over cocktails.

But the larger, more painful paradoxes were harder to reconcile. We all wondered about the connection, if any, to the Oklahoma City bombing. Had the greater treachery triggered this man's demons and manifested itself all over again by claiming yet another life? Or had the stalker isolated himself to such a degree that he was not aware of the carnage on April 19, just horribly in sync with the day's upheaval—and the evening's storms? I would learn to live beyond these questions, but it would take time.

Later that spring I found myself in front of Grandma's house again. Her azaleas were blooming, and I stopped to admire them from the curb. I'd never met the new owners, so couldn't invite myself inside to revisit memories. Even the azaleas seemed strangely off limits. The morning paper was to the east of the walk, and I thought about getting out of the car, tossing it gently on the porch, and sneaking a closer look at the flower beds in the process. But who knew what curiosities, perhaps fears, my harmless intentions might provoke? So I drove away with that neighborly gesture, and other notions of goodwill, still stirring my imagination.

My grandmother and grandfather Miller made
numerous road trips during their fifty-plus years
of marriage. Grandma especially loved to go to
fairs and carnivals.

I'm always a little uncomfortable with this 1950 photo of Grandma and Grandpa Crane, shot in their furniture store. Clearly
they were on different sides of the aisle, even before my mother's
death.

(Opposite) Since I don't have any firsthand
memories of my mother, it's hard for me to
imagine her in an everyday context. I think
of her as the sixteen-year-old in this studio
picture—without any sort of backdrop.

Wesley, my father, couldn't really be at ease unless he was "in uniform." He never saw combat during World War II, but he did experience battle fatigue on the home front.

Grandma Crane made sure I learned to read before I started to school, so I wouldn't ever feel trapped. My favorite book during those early years was a collection of Mother Goose tales.

My brother, Mark, tried to trick the camera and hide the fact that our dog, Tuffy, was missing an eye.

In this publicity photo for *Remnants of Glory*, I still believed that catfish had scales.

Earl Hamner warned me about the dangers of "the recipe" as we prepared for this *Writing Out Loud* interview in 2006. The show's director, Gary Johns, is in the foreground. Photograph by Casey Morgan.

Roger Rosenblatt, Amy Tan (with Lilli), Billie Letts, and I got to enjoy a few moments together during the 2004 Celebration of Books. Photograph courtesy of *The Tulsa World*.

Basically my job, as seen here, is to focus on other writers and artists, while fading into the background myself. In this photo, I was going over program notes for the 2002 Celebration of Books with Elizabeth Forsythe Hailey, Doug Marlette, and actress Marsha Mason. Photograph by David Varmecky.

Jim Lehrer, Kate Lehrer, and Lee Cullum shared their thoughts about literature and writing at the 2000 Celebration of Books. Jim moderated the first presidential debate between George W. Bush and Al Gore just a few days later. Photograph by David Varmecky.

I could be worse employed
Than as a watcher of the void,
Whose part should be to tell
What star if any fell.

—Robert Frost, "On Making Certain
Anything Has Happened"

Even though I grew up in a small town, I was always getting lost. "Mostly it's because her head's in the clouds," Wesley tried to explain. "She has one of those overactive imaginations." He usually made these pronouncements in hushed tones, as if I were suffering from some sort of glandular condition. Finally he settled on the euphemism preoccupied. If I wound up in Wagoner on my way to Muskogee, it was because I was preoccupied. Preoccupied *with stories*. Preoccupied *with dreams. Just plain* preoccupied.

In Tahlequah, at least, Grandma had been able to teach me how to locate myself by referring to the people and values we had in common. That's how she'd first given me directions to the grocery store, never resorting to vague notions of east or west, just patiently sending me first to Mrs. Wilson's house, from there to Mrs. Campbell's house, and then finally across the street to Safeway. Maps like that were lived, not followed.

During one of my early trips to New York, I once became so buoyed by the sense of being at home as a writer that I decided to venture out on my own. My newfound confidence was quickly put to the test, though, when I found myself in an unsettling part of town. I say "unsettling," because I'd seen a storefront sign proclaiming, EAR PIERCING WITH OR WITHOUT PAIN, *and the proprietor charged more for pain. Clearly I was lost, and I couldn't find a taxi—or a phone booth.*

My only recourse was to purchase a Star Map from a vendor hawking his wares on the street corner. The map was of little use to anyone without my particular shortcomings, for it only detailed the locations of celebrity homes. But recalling Grandma's early people maps to the grocery store, I used Yoko Ono's apartment and Katharine Hepburn's brownstone as coordinates to find my way back again.

Star Maps

When Wesley drove to Tulsa to attend a friend's funeral, he knew only that the service would be held at a chapel on Peoria, which was pretty specific information by Tahlequah standards. After he arrived, he was especially glad he'd come, because apparently none of Roger's other old friends had been able to make the trip. It wasn't until the minister asked mourners to bow their heads—in memory of Reba Mae Washington—that Wesley realized he was at the wrong funeral. At that point, he felt honor-bound to stay and told Reba's family during the viewing that, even though he'd never met Reba personally, he would miss her.

〜

One night, on my way home from work, it was raining so heavily, I accidentally got off at the Chouteau exit, thinking it was the entrance to the Cherokee Turnpike. I was disoriented at first, trying to locate myself with unexpected storefronts and traffic lights. It wasn't until I pulled into a convenience store that I realized where I was—in the stalker's hometown. In fact I was close enough to his mother's house for my mind to get tangled in crime-scene tape. But I needed gas and I was hungry. So I overcame any squeamishness, filled the car's tank, and bought a candy bar. I had a longer trip to make.

I even resisted the ghoulish temptation to drive down what I'd heard was a "normal" country lane, where every home, except the mother's, would be bright with the business of preparing meals and catching up on the day's laundry. Naturally I was curious, but I realized how risky it was to feed my imagination. I'd already speculated about the scary possibilities beyond this Amish community, known for its horse-drawn carriages and homemade cheese. The challenge for me was to focus on particulars—timelines, affidavits, forensic evidence—just to keep this single crime from overreaching itself in my psyche.

According to the newspapers, the man had decided to disregard his lawyer's advice and plead guilty to spare his family additional pain. They, in turn, had publicly forgiven *him,* but not his actions. The only "closure" for anyone came with the judge's sentence—life without parole—but the ruling carried its own irony. The killer/stalker entered prison just as Mark was being released early for good behavior.

Wesley immediately secured a job for Mark doing construction work, and though Mark embraced his new responsibilities admirably, relations continued to be strained between all of us. Unlike the stalker's family, we were struggling with levels of forgiveness, perhaps because we were free agents still capable of hurting each other. Wesley himself indirectly addressed our problems with legal counsel he gave to Lori. Lori had received a traffic ticket she wanted to dispute, but Wesley cautioned her, all of us, by advising, "Honey, you're guilty. You don't want *justice;* you want *mercy.*"

As a family, we needed to learn how to be *merciful* with each other. Wesley and I especially were trying to come to terms with our early history, but it was difficult for us to focus on my stepmother's abuse, except as a side issue in less substantial arguments. He'd recall the Christmas I'd given him an electric toothbrush, right after his teeth had been pulled—he liked to equate this to bringing roller skates to an amputee. Then suddenly, out of nowhere, he'd blurt that he'd never been physically abusive with me himself, though he did confess off-handedly that he'd been my stepmother's accessory "after the fact."

These were troublesome memories, and we should have been sorting through them with trained therapists, but it never occurred to us to get outside help. Even in 1990s Tahlequah, mental health care was considered the last and most embarrassing option—for individuals who were so disturbed that old-timers referred to them as *off*. If, God forbid, entire families sought treatment, then the prevailing view was that they simply weren't committed enough to resolving their own problems. We'd already used too many harsh words with each other to fret over dismissive labels, even *off*, but we couldn't bear the public stigma of having failed each other.

So rather than scheduling appointments to address our dysfunction in cozy offices with overstuffed pillows, we'd unexpectedly lock grocery carts in the aisles of Safeway, not so *safe* for us, and assail each other with angry endearments. Wesley liked to refer to me as *T. M.*, short for *troublemaker*. And I'd stumbled upon the perfect handle for him, after spraying Coke on his Lincoln at the Not-a-Spot carwash and announcing, "I've had it with you, Buster." I'd expected him to act as a human shield for the car—the Lincoln was precious to him—but instead he'd inadvertently betrayed his weakness by demanding, and I'd never seen him so fierce, "Don't you ever call me *Buster*."

To him, being his father's namesake validated his own life, and he also prided himself on the incidental cachet of being linked to the great theologian John Wesley. This double distinction had been slightly compromised after Grandma Miller's nursing home admission that the name was *partly* an homage to one of her ancestors, the nefarious outlaw John Wesley Hardin. But whatever associations Grandma had actually attached to *Wesley*, it did give her son a sense of importance that made him especially vulnerable to my indiscriminate use of *Buster*.

Maintaining his image wasn't just a matter of ego with him; it was his discipline. When he'd been recovering from cancer, he'd regained his strength by standing before a mirror and struggling to knot his tie correctly. He'd even adjusted to an artificial bladder by having his suits retailored so he could address a jury without revealing the bulge of his new infirmities. And, like Uncle Alton, he'd continued to make weekly visits to the barbershop, proving to himself and everyone else that his hair was still tenaciously black—with only flecks of gray.

In other words, he could button down, polish, and comb-over his shortcomings in such a way that he sometimes deluded himself, especially as he got older. Though he'd always been remarkably generous as an attorney, providing free legal services for all war veterans, other clients began to take advantage of him. He let one local businessman walk out of the office without paying, because he'd initially thought the man was just too embarrassed to talk about fees with someone of his stature.

It was only after my stepmother Louise's death that he began to recognize the same ordinariness in himself that he'd always seen in everyone else. Louise had shielded him from the mundane to such an extent that he was barely functional without her. To his credit, he tried to manage, but he put laundry detergent in the dishwasher, called neighbors to find out where to buy coffee, and even got duped by Mark into thinking his latest discovery, aluminum foil, was actually sold in specialty shops.

He wasn't truly humbled, though, until he needed work done at his office and stopped by a new law firm to ask the receptionist if the young attorneys had someone to wash their windows. After getting him a cup of coffee, she explained that they'd just hired a woman that morning, but she encouraged him to check back in a couple of weeks to see if they had another opening. This was the equivalent of a Tahlequah epiphany, for he realized that the expensive suit and overall look just weren't working anymore. He'd been pegged as a window washer.

Even he could appreciate the irony at first, but afterwards he seemed to be besieged by all of his other mistaken identities, including the most baffling one of all, being recognized as a father.

᳁

A bear ventured into town one spring, causing widespread speculation. A few people thought he'd escaped from a circus, because he was so cunning. He'd even been photographed washing himself in a tub full of rainwater. But most believed he was from the Arkansas hills and had chased his prey so far beyond the border that he'd become disoriented by city lights, the reason he'd run at full speed across the university campus before finally disappearing—just in time. One hunter was trying to shoot him, claiming that if Tahlequah made an exception for one lost bear, it would be an open invitation to others, some of them vicious.

᳁

When I was five, Grandma Crane had taken Mark and me to the circus, and we returned home overly indulged in cotton candy, much too restless to go to bed. Wesley and my young stepmother had binged as well—on alcohol—and Wesley had passed out for the evening, so we were pretty much left to our own devices until we finally fell asleep. At some point, I suddenly awoke, screaming from a nightmare about wolves, only to discover that my stepmother was the real-life shadow looming over me. Speechless with anger, she grabbed the one weapon available to her, a hardcover book, and began beating me, until I passed out, too.

The next morning when Sally arrived for work, she alerted Wesley. Apparently, my back was black with bruises, and Wesley was so afraid that I couldn't walk that he kept trying to coax me to my feet. I was too paralyzed with fear to respond and wouldn't approach him, until he promised that I could still spend the day at Grandma Crane's playing with my cousins. However, he did set one condition: this would have to be our secret, or someone could get killed. He issued a similar warning to Sally, who acquiesced with a stipulation of her own—she wasn't about to become the Miller family's scapegoat.

Though Wesley did express concern for my physical well-being, he made no attempt to take me to the hospital or even phone the doctor. Instead, he contacted a friend of his at a local pharmacy and asked him to send over a prescription for broad-spectrum antibiotics. He also forced me to chew a couple of baby aspirins and cautioned me again that, no matter what, I had to act as if nothing had happened—a significant challenge, even for Jeanne Crain's daughter.

That's how I spent the day, smiling for my life, for all of our lives, until Grandma insisted that I take a bath. As always, she tested the water for me, but she became suspicious when I told her I was suddenly too embarrassed to let her see me naked. She remembered aloud that I'd been wincing throughout the afternoon and suddenly started examining me. Earlier, during a bathroom break, I'd tried to twist enough to see my injuries in the mirror, but I'd been too sore. I did see them, though, in Grandma's eyes as she sank to the floor, saying only, "My dear God." At first, I claimed that I'd fallen the night before, but she knew better. She knew *worse*.

Her first thought was to contact the authorities. Except Wesley and Grandpa Miller *were* the authorities, and she knew she could never get custody in their jurisdiction. Besides, I'd become hysterical, begging her not to let anyone else know. She did, of course, tell Grandpa Crane, and when they joined forces to challenge Wesley, he swore that he'd already taken steps to make sure my stepmother could never hurt me again. By that, they just assumed that he'd sent her back to her family in Tulsa, but she remained in the house for the next two years.

My grandparents realized all over again how much losing their daughter had cost them. Sometimes I'd look out the window at night and see their car circling the house, but they were careful not to provoke any more tension. As Lori once put it, they were fine people, but their trust in decency failed them. So Grandma and I didn't cover quite as much territory in her Buick as we should have. We'd driven our way through death, negligence, and abandoned dreams, but we'd bypassed the harsher reality of deliberate meanness.

For his part, Wesley immediately presented me with early Christmas gifts, supposedly from my stepmother, but I was growing up fast enough to recognize his distinctive writing on the gift tags. It was also obvious that he'd come to some sort of understanding with her. Even in our midsized house, Mark and I rarely saw her and depended on Sally to take care of our basic needs. Though I had mostly recovered from the physical injuries, I was emotionally traumatized. I kept fixating on ways to entice Jeanne Crain back into my life and subsequently developed a basic distrust of everyone I'd relied on in the past.

During the next few months I became so fearful of being poisoned that I refused to eat food prepared by family members until someone else test-tasted it first. I also slept with a doll wedged over my stomach—a protective shield in case my stepmother tried to stab me. I'd never been threatened in these ways, but once my safety zone had been breached, it was easy to imagine being violated on an even greater scale, and I longed for an escape. Any time I was in the car with Grandma, I asked her why we couldn't just drive forever. She never answered me directly, but when she swallowed obligatory bites of my sandwiches, I knew she was asking herself the same question.

Sally was the one who finally went to Grandma Miller with the truth, but only after my stepmother had forced Wesley to fire her because of another dispute. As it turned out, Grandma Miller had been secretly bankrolling Sally for years, so she deftly manipulated her into revealing enough grisly details to force my stepmother out of town before sundown. That had been the proverbial deadline Grandma Miller had set for her, and she hadn't minimized the threat by brokering it through Wesley. She'd called her directly and explained the "or else" alternative so convincingly that the woman never returned to Tahlequah.

It wasn't until after *Remnants* was published that Grandma Miller began sharing more details about the incident with me. Since I'd included a sex scene in the novel, she'd become convinced I was finally ready for an adult-to-adult confession. Though she'd kept Uncle Alton on standby that day, she'd fully intended to do the deed herself, stabbing my stepmother in the back and then leaving it to the public to speculate about unknown assailants. Her only reason for issuing a deadline had been as a matter of convenience—she'd needed time to line up an alibi, playing hymns on the piano with her sister.

Her decision to confide in me, she said, wasn't to make me feel beholden, though she was relieved I'd learned to eat with gusto again. Instead she had something "scary" to tell me: no one ever really rescued us; we ultimately had to rescue ourselves. That's why she wanted to warn me that I still had other obstacles to overcome. Naturally she was devoted to Wesley and Mark—they were her offspring, too—but she cautioned me not to enable them by setting aside my own needs. That's just what she'd done with Alton, and as she approached the end of her life, she was realizing—too late—that she'd undermined him and herself.

As flattered as I was to be the confidante of her latter years, I wasn't ready yet to be her granddaughter. I learned that the night I got a call from her retirement center telling me she'd been rushed to the hospital. The doctor had already made his diagnosis by the time I arrived. She'd suffered a massive stroke and wouldn't last until morning. However, right before she'd lapsed into a coma, she'd asked about her family, and he'd told her I was on the way. "That's good," she'd replied—with every confidence that I could help her through this final transition.

And I tried to be dutiful, as she clung to me with such tenacity that she scratched through layers of memory—and regret. Wesley was in Hawaii, and Mark couldn't be reached, so eventually I had to make a hard decision for all of us, including Grandma Miller, by gently prying her fingers from mine and letting her go. Even so, I continued to stay with her until she suddenly had one last convulsion. Then I cowered, giving up my last moments with her to bolt into the hall and call for a nurse's help.

Grandma Miller herself would have been the first to understand. I would have to negotiate some other dark passages—with a former lover, the stalker, and an ever-elusive dream—before I could see the light of her room again. But it was too late to reclaim the place I'd relinquished that night and to rethink the words I should have said then. The only way left for me to still be mindful of her was to acknowledge the stands she'd taken in her life and to be just as vigilant on my own behalf.

All of which is to say that I cornered Wesley in his living room one Sunday, cut through the banter and innuendo, and asked him straight out why he hadn't been more protective of Mark and me following the beating. The reference to Mark surprised him, though Mark had tried to tell us what it had been like for him as a three-year-old—silently running circles during the attack and, afterwards, living with the fear that such a thing could happen again, not to him, but to me. Sometimes being spared could be hurtful.

But Wesley had more immediate concerns on his mind and was wedging towels under the front door to block out drafts. After Louise's death, he'd remarried and was going through another divorce, so he was sensitive to any unexpected "cold fronts." Still, he had an answer for me, one he warned that I wouldn't like—he'd wanted to avoid the gossip. *Gossip* wasn't a big enough word to cover the breach between us, but if he was remorseful, he didn't show it; he'd stood stone-faced before too many juries to waver in front of his daughter. Instead he directed a question at me— didn't I remember the way it had been—nosy neighbors dropping by unannounced, operators listening in on our phone conversations?

I did recall one operator in particular who'd read in the local paper that I was performing in a piano recital. She asked me to play "Silent Night" for her over the telephone, and Grandma had held up the receiver like a microphone. Of course *we'd* had nothing to hide.

Wesley, though, at least according to him, had come in for harsher scrutiny, and one "vicious" rumor had even accused him of getting Mother pregnant after doctors had warned them that childbirth could kill her. Another widely circulated story had supposedly claimed that he'd been having an extramarital affair at the time of Mother's death. So just imagine, he speculated, what would have happened if word had gotten out earlier about the child abuse. We might never have been able to solve our problems and be the kind of family that—

Went to prison, resorted to drugs, and *kept violent secrets.* In fact, we shared so many characteristics with the stalker and his family, including my fear of being poisoned, that it was humbling to consider just what had saved us. But I didn't need to interrupt Wesley with these reminders. He knew the only reason we were even having this conversation after thirty years was because the anodynes we'd relied on were finally exhausting themselves—his prescriptions were about to expire, and I'd run out of fiction.

When Lori's sister Rosemary was visiting from Florida,
she and Lori took the turnpike to see their brother Phil.
It was dark by the time they started home, and they
stopped at McDonald's, the midway point between
Tulsa and Oklahoma City, for some coffee. Once they
were on the road again, they told family stories to make
the miles go faster. They'd been driving for at least an
hour before they realized they'd gotten turned around
and were backtracking. Of course they could have gone
a little farther, spent the night at Phil's, and told even
more stories, but they had so many other responsibili-
ties that away seemed closer.

~

He had wanted to avoid the gossip. The fact that I'd never
been able to trust Wesley was part of what made him so
intriguing to me. One summer he publicly joined ranks
against me in a zoning dispute, and Jonathan felt so betrayed on my behalf that he left a note on my dresser saying, "I'm always on your side." I'd already given up on
getting that kind of unconditional support from Wesley,
but he had been an inspiration of sorts—I'd had to learn
how to be inventive just so I could hold my own with him.

We also shared an appreciation of literature, and whenever he'd give me a book—I especially recall *The Complete
Poems of Emily Dickinson*—he'd sign it over to me, almost
as if it were some sort of arbitration agreement. "I apolo-
gize to thee / For thine own Duplicity," he'd say bending
Dickinson to make his point, and I'd reply, "Ourself, behind
ourself concealed, / Should startle most." This kind of banter had become our backup language for special occasions,
because we were just as awkward with our endearments as
we were with our grievances; it was easier to let the books
we exchanged do the talking for us.

Like me, Wesley wasn't just drawn to books but also to
the people who wrote them, and he'd had some significant

author experiences of his own. He'd listened to Vachel Lindsey recite the "The Congo"—in Tahlequah of all places—shortly before the poet had committed suicide. Hearing Lindsey, he said, and picking up on his rhythms had changed the cadences of his life forever. And he loved to tell about the time he'd attended a reading by Robert Frost. During the question-and-answer portion of that program, he'd asked Frost what he'd meant by repeating the last line, "and miles to go before I sleep," in "Stopping by Woods on a Snowy Evening." Frost had reportedly replied, "Not a damn thing."

His most memorable encounters, though, were with political icons, particularly his idol, former president Harry Truman. He'd actually gotten to spend an afternoon with Truman in his presidential library in Independence. I'm not sure how he was able to arrange such a meeting, probably through some of his political friends, but he did use the unlikely visit to pass along a peculiar life lesson: almost anyone I could think of, no matter how famous, was more accessible to me than I realized—except for Wesley himself.

It was general knowledge that he'd never been one to show up at school plays or parent-teacher conferences. However, his special interests and parental instincts occasionally overlapped in surprising ways. During my teenage years, he presented me with a collection of famous political photographs, all personally autographed. I was so overwhelmed by the attention that I dutifully displayed Lyndon Johnson's photo alongside my Beatles posters.

That said, I should note that there was also some compensation involved. He realized I was just indulging him and always made sure I had plenty of loose change so my friends and I could meet at the drugstore payphone and reach out to *our* favorite celebrities. We were occasionally successful, and when the local newspapers reported our long-distance visits with Marlo Thomas and Bill Cosby, Wesley saved the clippings.

He felt a similar pride about my work with the Center and talked strategy with me when I decided to relocate the program to Tulsa. I'd asked for his legal advice, wondering if Rogers State could block the move. Though he didn't give me an immediate answer, he phoned me after midnight one evening to tell me not to worry. He was convinced that school administrators wouldn't challenge me outside their jurisdiction. As he put it, "Small ships need to stay close to shore."

The late-night call was unusual for him, but I knew he was struggling to get off the sedatives that he had used for decades to short-circuit his regrets. Since the early 1960s he'd been addicted to Placidyl, Equanil, and Tuinal, which he'd chased with rum to maximize the effect. Many nights during what he'd referred to as the "Kennedy-Johnson years" he'd passed out in front of the television set, leaving it up to Mark, Louise, and me to wrestle his dead weight and get him to bed. Fortunately he'd given up alcohol almost effortlessly right before his cancer surgery, but in the process he'd become even more reliant on prescription drugs.

One Friday Mark contacted me at work to say that he'd visited with Wesley's urologists, who'd told him that Wesley's dialysis, one of the consequences of his life-saving operations, wasn't working. The sedatives were lowering his blood pressure to such an extent that his blood couldn't circulate through the machines properly. They had tried talking with him, but he wasn't listening and would get prescriptions from other doctors if they threatened to cut back on his supply.

He had wanted to avoid the gossip. The line kept replaying in my mind's ear like a bad song lyric, but I agreed to stop by Wesley's house the next morning and discuss possible rehab options. Even as I rang the bell, I was preparing to remind him that he'd championed similar treatments for Mark, but he didn't answer, and I started knocking instead. My first thought was that he'd probably barricaded the doors with towels again, muffling the sound, but I also worried that he'd fallen—or worse.

I was still knocking, banging, when the city police arrived and told me Wesley had called them. "He thought that I was a burglar," I said, making a mental note to phone ahead next time. But the officer, a distant cousin, looked embarrassed and explained that Wesley had reported me for "creating a disturbance." I didn't have to explain that I'd meant no harm—he could see that—but he was obviously confused by this level of distrust between a father and his daughter. He reddened all over again when he let it slip that *he* had a key to his parents' house.

However, he promised to persuade Wesley not to file any charges and suggested that perhaps we could work out our differences over the phone. I did call repeatedly throughout the day but always got a busy signal and didn't want to upset him even more by trying to visit him in person again. All of his family members and friends felt the same way. That was the crisis Wesley had brought upon himself. By locking the world out, he'd locked himself in, and suddenly his life was at stake. As Emily Dickinson had said—in the book Wesley had signed with such authority—"Doom is the House without the Door."

❧

One day my ex-lover and I wound up directly across from each other at a four-way stop, and neither one of us wanted to make the first move. It had been three months since I'd last seen him, so I was glad he recognized the impasse for what it was. Cars had lined up in back of us and were honking impatiently, as if we were

holding up a processional. But I didn't want us to meet
going in opposite directions, so I turned right and kept
turning right until I was lost in the country. Or thought
I was, until I saw a teenage couple I knew returning
from some remote lovers' lane. Then I turned left and
kept turning left until I was back home.

~

A few days later another cousin was getting her hair fixed
and found out that Wesley and his wife had reconciled—at
least temporarily, though they still weren't living together.
As an aside, she also let me know that the local beauty operators were firmly in my camp and wanted to do all they
could to be supportive, including scheduling me in at the
last minute whenever I needed a trim. The fact that I'd
stayed in Tahlequah, even after I'd started working in Tulsa,
had convinced everyone that all my earlier grumblings
about moving to New York had simply been, as one beauti-
cian put it, "a hormonal thing."

Nevertheless, the Center itself was thriving at Oklahoma State University in Tulsa. The metropolitan base had
already extended our outreach and was making it much
easier to attract high profile speakers. So even though my
dreams hadn't taken me everywhere I'd wanted to go, I'd
been given a rare opportunity to reel in the horizon and ex-
plore some reverse means of transit—by bringing some of
my favorite authors to Oklahoma. Our first Tulsa incarnation of the Celebration of Books was going to feature old
friends like Jim Lehrer, Elizabeth Forsythe Hailey, and Joyce
Carol Thomas, as well as scores of Oklahoma authors. I'd
also managed to book Earl Hamner, creator of *The Waltons*,
and Ronnie Claire Edwards, who'd played Corabeth on the
series.

I'd gotten in touch with Ronnie Claire, a native Oklahoman, and Earl through Betsy Hailey, and I was ecstatic.
After years of defying Grandma by watching *The Waltons*

clandestinely, I was finally going public with my love for this television family that had listened to John Boy read his novel aloud—and then served him southern fried delicacies to keep him inspired. But I'd lived beyond that fantasy myself. Mid-life stress was catching up with me, and during one of our phone visits, I told Earl that I was hoping he'd bring me a bottle of "the recipe." As hard as it was for Earl to turn down anyone, he finally said, "Darling, I just don't think that would be a good idea. It's so much stronger than wine, you see."

In the midst of all these conference calls and preparations, my stepmother phoned one morning to tell me that Wesley was suffering from kidney failure and that she was driving him to a Tulsa hospital. She was understandably anxious as she undertook the trip—he'd refused to come by ambulance—so I promised to make all of the hospital arrangements for them. Even as we talked, I was jotting down the hospital numbers from the yellow pages, and I contacted the admissions office immediately.

At first I was surprised that the woman answered the phone, "Laureate," but in my frenzy just assumed that the hospital was going for a more personal approach by using first names. I gave her mine, then told her Wesley, "an emergency case," was en route and would be arriving in about two hours. I also made sure she had his other account information and asked her to especially watch out for my stepmother, since she, too, was under so much pressure.

I checked with "Laureate" again in two hours, but Wesley still hadn't been admitted. So we started touching base then at thirty-minute intervals, and "Laureate" alerted aids throughout the facility to be on the lookout for him. During our last exchange, "Laureate" admitted that she and the staff were growing increasingly concerned and wanted to know what the actual diagnosis was beyond "really serious." When I told her kidney failure, she explained in a voice that was a little too soothing for my tastes that Laureate was a psychiatric clinic.

In the meantime, my stepmother and Wesley had managed to find their way to the proper hospital, where he'd been treated and released for continued outpatient therapy in Tahlequah. However, he had already received messages from the law office that I'd inadvertently registered him at Laureate, and he was furious, refusing to believe that I'd "committed" him accidentally. But his anger served him well. His blood pressure became elevated just enough to make dialysis more viable, and I was free to focus on the Celebration.

Our guests began arriving within the next few days, and a friend and I went to the airport to pick up Earl. I'd just met Ronnie Claire, who was nothing like the staid character she'd portrayed on the series. Quite the contrary—she was flamboyant, anxious in a charming sort of way, and dangerously witty. Earl, on the other hand, was exactly as I'd pictured him. Though the airline had lost his luggage, he was busy thanking everyone from the ticket agents to the customer service representatives for giving him the opportunity to buy a new wardrobe during his visit.

In addition to introducing the Waltons to Oklahoma, I was also looking forward to honoring Joyce Thomas for her ongoing contributions to children's literature. *Abysinnia*, the musical adaptation of her novel, *Marked by Fire*, was playing in various venues around the country, and the composers had given their permission for Ernestine Dillard to sing "Honey and Lemon," one of their signature songs, at the Celebration. Ernestine had reached out to the entire country with her riveting rendition of "God Bless America" during the memorial service for victims of the Oklahoma City bombing, and I knew she had the range—of voice and spirit—to capture the honey/lemon dynamic of Joyce's work.

So we were all set on opening night. The grand piano was positioned strategically at the front of the concert hall we'd rented, and Ernestine was warming up backstage. Lonnie, her pianist, was in place at the piano; Joyce was in the wings ready to recite a poem; and I was reviewing my opening remarks. We were in sync, and I could already feel the crowd's anticipation. This was going to be a special moment—for Joyce, for all of us. Except that one of my coworkers was tugging at me frantically. The piano was locked, and the only person who had the key was out of town.

Basically, we had two choices—we could wheel in an upright through the middle of the crowd or send for a locksmith. Since it was a Friday night, no one knew how long it might take to get the locksmith, so the upright seemed like the best solution. I would, though, have to let the audience know what was happening, and I felt the agenda I'd been holding crumple as I approached the podium. The program, I explained, as I looked out at our noted guests and saw Jim Lehrer smiling, would continue, though there might be some slight distractions—like a piano winding its way through the aisles.

Apparently it's not so easy to move a piano, even on wheels, but the technical crew was sensitive to the situation and tried to be discreet by creaking forward a few feet at a time whenever our speakers received a round of applause. Jim's award presentation to Betsy and Ronnie Claire's storytelling advanced the piano close enough to actually bring Ernestine out on stage and let her warm up directly in front of the audience. But Lonnie was already waving his concern and stopped Ernestine midscale. The upright was out of tune and several of its strings were broken.

It was at that point I suddenly remembered the entire evening was being taped for our archives, and I made one of the most critical decisions of my career, announcing to the packed house and to posterity that we *were* sending for a locksmith after all. So exit Ernestine and enter Earl Hamner, and then Joyce. Joyce's reading was out of sequence, preceding Ernestine, but we had to fill the gaps, and I'd been resorting to every anecdote I could think of just to keep from losing our momentum, such as it was. Even as the locksmith marched into our midst with a huge pair of bolt cutters, I was trying to distract the crowd and offended our hosts by asking why they'd even locked the piano in the first place—"Did they think someone was going to break in and play a song?"

But the locksmith had become our star for the evening, holding up his bolt cutters for all of us to applaud and then freeing the piano with one broad stroke. In the meantime, Lonnie rushed to the keyboard for a test refrain and gave Ernestine the go-ahead. Since she'd already warmed up twice, she dispensed with the preliminaries and eased right into "Honey and Lemon," building to a resounding crescendo that had the entire crowd on its feet. We finally had our moment. Voices, lyrics, and circumstances had culminated in a way that highlighted Joyce's theme—life as a mix of honey and lemon, emphasis on *honey*. Joyce would later write about what that convergence had meant to her.

It was Earl Hamner, though, who gave us closure for the occasion by standing up in the audience and saying "Goodnight, everyone," with the rich Virginia accent we'd heard so many times introducing *The Waltons*. As one of my friends told me later, I wasn't just championing literature, I was bringing back vaudeville.

✺

During one of our Celebrations, before cell phones, I got word that Jim Lehrer was missing. His wife, Kate, a noted novelist, had arrived earlier and had planned to rendezvous with him at the hotel. But Jim was over two hours late. In the meantime I'd received another message—Kate was missing—and the double mystery

wasn't solved until the Lehrers bumped into each other
in a hotel corridor. The hotel had been trying to protect
their privacy and had accidentally booked them in
separate rooms. It was something we'd think about
over cocktails, how people could be so close and still not
realize it.

～

Thanks to the success of the Celebration and the support of the university, *Writing Out Loud* found its way to OETA, Oklahoma's PBS affiliate, which gave the show its first statewide audience. I should emphasize that even with the expanded outreach, the show was still a low-budget operation. Though we did have the capacity to shoot on location, we would need to tape a series of interviews in each venue to keep the program cost effective. In other words, we were basically "live to tape," which meant we only got to edit out major gaffes and were often so overwhelmed that we somehow overlooked them. Shortly after I did an interview with my friend Joe Carter, a former White House press secretary and a leading authority on Will Rogers, I started getting calls that my slip had been showing throughout the program.

On at least two occasions, a substitute camera operator either forgot to turn on a camera or neglected to focus it properly. One of the interviews was with Texas novelist Kathy Hepinstall, author of *The House of Gentle Men*. Gary, my director, explained that the footage of Kathy and the two of us together was fine, but the camera on me had been turned off during my questions. The fix, absolutely necessary in this case, would require that I wear the same clothes and retape all my portions of the interview, which would have been easy enough if I hadn't already donated my suit to Goodwill. I tried to buy it back from the charity, but the clerks could only locate the skirt. That meant the only option left for us was to get as close to the original look as possible and then hope no one would spot the difference.

Another time, I'd arranged what for me was a real coup. I was going to do a show with the legendary portrait artist Charles Banks Wilson in Tulsa's Gilcrease Musuem, known for its prized collection of western art. The museum had even agreed to open up its vaults, giving us unprecedented access to Wilson's work. So we couldn't have had a better venue for my first meeting with Charles, and we developed an easy rapport with each other as he talked about what he referred to as "pigments of the imagination." He also shared delightful stories about painting Thomas Hart Benton from life and socializing in New York with Oklahoma expatriates Lynn Riggs and Woody Guthrie.

It was a week later when Gary called with the bad news—one camera had been out of focus. This was particularly embarrassing since Charles had insisted on coming to Gilcrease and doing the interview, even though he'd had a minor car accident en route. But we did get some honey to go with our lemon—the production studio agreed to subsidize a trip to Wilson's home in Arkansas, so we could do a new interview with him surrounded by his personal art collection. And, thankfully, the cameras just couldn't get enough of Charles and his work during that shoot. We photographed his early sketches of Benton, his portrait of Will Rogers, and a series of paintings he'd done of pure-blood Indians.

Since he was so open to us and to our questions, I decided to violate his privacy even more by asking to see his studio. I'd imagined that it would be as perfectly aligned as his sketches of personalities like Jim Thorpe that were sectioned off to make sure the components were as precise as possible. But the studio itself, lined by smudged windows, seemed to be in disarray with a collection of easels, works in progress—one of historian Angie Debo—and piles of paint tubes, squeezed from the middle.

Later, he took us for fried chicken, and as he continued to speak about his work and his connections with literary friends like Langston Hughes, he described himself as a storyteller. In fact, that's why he was redoing the portrait of Debo. After attending a panel about her at the Celebration of Books, he'd decided that his official capitol portrait of her wasn't warm enough, so he was repainting her with a red sweater to reveal her personal attributes. That's when his studio began to make sense to me. Charles lived from the gut, from the bulge of his colors, and then, upon reflection, found precision in his brush strokes.

Through the years we had even more challenges and misunderstandings with the show. When we were taping Choctaw storyteller Tim Tingle in the lobby of a car dealership, one of our sponsors, he agreed to sing "Amazing Grace" for us in Choctaw. By Tim's countenance, it was clear that this wasn't just a performance for him; he was spiritually in tune with the hymn and didn't even look askance at the Mercedes in back of us when a voice came over the public address system telling one of the salesmen he needed to report to the credit department. Luckily our microphones were so sound specific that the background announcement wasn't noticeable to anyone but us.

I hold myself directly responsible for the misunderstandings I alluded to earlier, because one of the challenges of producing a show is trying to anticipate problems ahead of time. One season we'd arranged to do a set of programs in the state capitol, one with Scout Cloud Lee, who'd starred for a season in the *Survivor* television series, which placed contestants in primitive conditions to see who could hold out the longest. Scout had been a runner-up and had since written a new book, *Sworn to Fun*. We'd visited about the show ahead of time, and I'd suggested she bring some of her mementos from *Survivor*—her hand-carved toothbrush, her coconut bowl, and other novelties.

When she didn't show up at the appointed time, we were a little concerned, but then she called to explain. She'd been detained by capitol police for having a machete in her satchel. Needless to say, I'd failed to mention the machete would be a no-go, but we were able to vouch for Scout and get her security clearance.

The show, though, that most touched my heart with its awkwardness and innocent inappropriateness was the one we did with Charles Chibitty, the last living Comanche code talker. Technically speaking, Charles wasn't a writer himself, but he'd been a favorite subject for historians, and it seemed only right that we do a featured interview with him. He was a true hero, who'd been on the beaches of Normandy on D-Day, transmitting messages to the Allies in his native tongue so the enemy couldn't intercept them. He often reminisced about how hard it had been to find Comanche expressions for the terminology of war. For instance, he and his fellow code talkers had used the Comanche name for *turtle* to communicate *tank*.

But in his old age, words were eluding him. He was confused when I came to pick him up and kept trying to clarify the clutter around him by pointing to a picture of his deceased wife, and then to a framed print of the Charles Banks Wilson painting *Freedom's Warrior*. Charles thought that *he* was the Indian soldier Wilson had depicted, but according to Wilson, he'd only been a model for the composite image. It didn't matter. Once we were in the car and began visiting about his work as a code talker, Charles came to life in his own right, and he was equally animated when we started taping, lapsing only occasionally.

We were halfway through the interview when I saw him reaching toward his face, and I wondered, at first, if he was uncomfortable in some way. I didn't have to wait long for an answer. Smiling coyly, he deftly slipped his false teeth from his mouth, dropped them into his shirt pocket and, just as adroitly, resumed our conversation. As I've noted, we rarely stopped taping because of the expense, so I did some quick budget calculations, trying to convince myself that, perhaps, no one would notice. That's when Charles rethought his decision, retrieved the teeth, and grinned to reinsert them. Even as we were finishing up the program, Gary and I had locked eyes in agreement. This would be one of those rare instances when we did edit.

Not that we had any notions of grandeur about our show. We were *local*, no question about it—the reason I'd often get voice messages, tagged urgent, wanting to know where a particular lady guest had gotten the sweater she was wearing—or, on a more profound level, why I'd never done an interview with Oprah. And I'd regularly run into viewers at the grocery store, or post office, or even more intimate settings—the underwear counter at Dillard's, for instance—who'd just want to say things like "That Kim Doner must be a lot of fun," or "P. C. Cast is so exotic."

Because *Writing Out Loud* had never just been about writing, though good books were our platform; mostly it was about finding ways to triumph over everyday life, whether it was learning how sportswriter Frank Deford had overcome the loss of his daughter, or how Anne Lamott had found religion, or even how Jane Smiley had managed to be so prolific while raising a family and enjoying her horses.

❧

Even though Grandma Crane had joined the Methodist church, she always thought of herself as a Baptist— sort of—because the distinction reminded her of her growing-up years in western Oklahoma. Being a Baptist then had meant being a Baptist everywhere. But there were so many different Baptist churches in Tahlequah that it confused her. Our Baptists didn't settle their disputes; they set up branch denominations based on singular convictions. You could dance with

one group, drink wine with another, and, if you were
truly "lost," could live an even fuller life by going from
church to church to suit your fancy.

~

As a child, I'd escaped the clutter and regret of Wesley's
living room by fantasizing about all the "regular" families
I watched as often as possible on television. I had adjusted
the fine-tuning to make the Nelsons more believable—and
fiddled with the vertical hold to keep the Cleavers from
bouncing beyond me. If, as Grandma Crane had predicted,
Smellevision had actually come to pass, I have no doubts
but what I could have overcome the lingering stench of rum
and cigar smoke to find a portal to Donna Reed's kitchen,
simply by tracking the scent of her apple pies, which were
always cooling before an open window.

So it was a peculiar reversal, the way television brought
me back *into* Wesley's living room and his life. After *Writing
Out Loud* became available in Tahlequah, he reestablished
contact with me on the pretext of discussing our guests.
He'd particularly keyed in to one of my early interviews
with Clifton Taulbert, who'd written a cultural memoir,
Once Upon a Time When We Were Colored.

Clifton's story suggesting that family support, at least in
part, could counterbalance discrimination had prompted
Wesley to suddenly take issue with Grandma Miller and
what he kept describing as her blatant racism. I didn't know
at the time that she'd persuaded him to break off his romance with the native woman in Hawaii, but I was encouraged to think that he'd finally developed a social conscience.
Like many Oklahomans of my generation, I was just learning about the 1921 Tulsa Race Riot, one of the worst riots
in our nation's history, and I'd done a series of television
interviews that showed just how calculating some of our
leaders had been in covering up the massacre.

I'd even requested an office overlooking the Greenwood District, the site of the riot, so I could keep it foremost in my mind as I planned future conferences. Even though the next Celebration wouldn't be until the following spring, I'd already booked Maya Angelou, a decision that seemed to please Wesley. His health continued to be frail, and I'd backed away from pressing him to resolve the breach between us. But sometimes, when were talking about Greenwood, I could hear undertones of personal remorse as he spoke about condoning violence by trying to pretend that it didn't exist. Not that he ever considered our family turmoil to be on the same level with large-scale atrocities, but in recognizing his own weaknesses, he'd become increasingly cynical about human nature in general.

He still declared himself to be a devout Methodist, but more and more, instead of quoting an occasional Bible verse, he'd reflect on the old Lucky Strikes cigarette slogan: "Nature in the Raw is Seldom Mild." And he knew that I had similar misgivings. Though I wasn't an atheist, which to me was a form of fundamentalism, I'd wavered from my earlier religious convictions and was an agnostic hoping for a reconfirmation of the beliefs I'd embraced as a child. I suspect that, as his life hung in the balance, he was looking for similar consolation.

One reason I believe that we'd become so enamored with celebrities was to counter our disillusionment. It was almost as if we were trying to replace the people we'd lost and might not see again with bigger-than-life personalities who would live forever—at least in our cultural memory. One day after the Sugar Bowl, he asked if I thought a field goal kicker who'd won the game in the closing seconds would be remembered for all time. Without thinking, I told him no, and it seemed to break his heart, not as a sports fan, but as an old man who wanted life to mean something beyond the moment.

A few weeks later, during the weekend of November 16, the date that had claimed the lives of both my mother and grandfather, Wesley had a heart attack and was transferred to a Tulsa hospital. We'd stayed in touch, but he called me at work one day and asked me to come see him that evening. He and my stepmother had separated again, and I knew it was a lonely time for him. One of the few comforts in his life was his deepening relationship with Mark. Though Mark's resources were limited, he'd been helping Wesley as much as he could by driving him to dialysis. Mark was genuinely anxious for him and had been conferring with some of my cousins and me about the possibility of assisted living.

Even though Wesley had been steadily declining for the past year, I was shocked to find him sustained by coils of tubes that made him look like a robotic version of himself. At first, he was reluctant to ask for my help, but he finally relented, motioning for me to raise his bed so he could speak from a sitting position. I noticed how fragile his grip was as I took his hand to ease him into a mound of pillows. Then he overcompensated, grabbing my arm so forcefully that I winced. *He'd wanted to avoid the gossip.* Those words still stood between us just as surely as the guardrails he kept readjusting. "I'm alone," he said, "and it's too late for me to do anything but to say that what I did was wrong, and I'm sorry."

This was all about that *mercy* he'd discussed with Lori, and I suddenly understood that for the first time in my life I was in control of our relationship. But I still felt vulnerable, even under these circumstances, and tried to distract him by pouring him a fresh glass of water and offering him a cup of Jello. "I finally finished *The Grapes of Wrath*," I told him, "and thought it was quite extraordinary. If you read it along with *Working Days*, you'll see that Steinbeck really admired the Joads—and Oklahoma—he . . ."

"You have to let it go," he said, and we both knew what

he meant. "As bad as it was, *you've got to let it go*—not for me, for your own sake. Otherwise this hurt is going to hold you back for the rest of your life and keep you from trusting anyone."

"I'll see you in Tahlequah," I said, leaning forward to give him a hug. Which was a beginning. Then I quoted Ma Joad, "All we got is the family unbroke," and he smiled.

❧

My great-aunt taught in one-room schoolhouses throughout Oklahoma, and at the end of each year, her students gave her their photos. By the time she retired, she'd collected hundreds of them and became so weary with remembering that she boxed them up and set them out with her trash. Later that day a middle-aged man rang her bell, handed the boxes to her, and introduced himself as one of her former students, now her garbage collector. Someone, he said, must have put her pictures out by mistake. So she thanked him and spent the rest of the day trying to place faces with specific schools. She'd driven many of the students to school herself, picking them up at their homes—in the middle of nowhere—and reaching each school child by child. But it was a confusing trip after so many years, so many miles, and she couldn't find the way anymore.

❧

Wesley did recover enough to return home and managed to make it out to Wal-Mart to purchase me one last gift, a receipt book that I'd needed to process registrations for the Celebration. Maya was proving to be a huge draw, and every time I filled in one of the blank forms, I'd feel like I was working out some sort of installment plan with him. But he died just a few days before the book festival, and, as I continued to drive back and forth to help my stepmother with the arrangements, I'd handle as much Celebration business as I could.

In my confusion, I'd given our authors a cell number that

was one digit off, and I'd already heard from the university that a Tulsa woman had called the main office complaining about getting crank calls from people claiming to be Earl Hamner, actress Mary Kay Place, and poet Joy Harjo.

I will always remember my conversation with Joy after I was finally able to reach her. She could hear the roar of the highway over the phone, and when I mentioned Wesley's death, she told me to "Hang in there." Joy was one of the most eloquent writers I'd ever met, and my favorite poem was "The Creation Story," in which she spoke of not having "the words / to carry a friend from her death / to the stars / correctly." She understood that no turn of phrase was poetic enough to account for loss, and she was right. I had to hang in there.

So one moment I was at Wesley's funeral, awkwardly holding hands with Mark, the next I was backstage at Tulsa's historic Brady Theater in the dressing room with Maya. She'd asked to see me, and I'd assumed she might have some concerns about the program. But instead, she wanted us to join hands for a blessing. I'd heard she wasn't feeling well, and she did look frail in her dressing gown, but when she hugged me, I was reassured by her strength.

And once she took the stage she was magnificent. The Ku Klux Klan had hidden out in the Brady during the race riots, but she reclaimed it that night when "Still I Rise" resonated throughout the theater and hundreds of African American women rose to their feet and wiped tears of triumph from their eyes. She went on to receive five standing ovations before slipping out the back door to avoid the press of the crowd, rushing toward the stage to present her with cookies, flowers, and poems. One of the things I admired most about Maya was that in spite of her great talent, she knew her limitations. The only gift we could really give her was to remember our time together, then let her exit gracefully so she could share with others.

It was several weeks later that I was going through some of Wesley's old correspondence and found the one letter he'd kept from Grandma Miller, perhaps as a reminder of the love she'd cost him. In it she was denouncing Martin Luther King and bemoaning the fact that she couldn't join those patriots taking to the streets of Atlanta to raise their fists against him. Of course I loved my grandmother and admired many of her better qualities, but she'd let prejudice diminish her—and Wesley. To my way of thinking, when Maya liberated us that evening, not just from social injustices but also from our own weaknesses, she delivered his eulogy.

∾

When I interviewed filmmaker Ken Burns in Still-water, I was responsible for getting him back to his bed and breakfast once we were finished. I'd planned to be at least a half-hour early so I could get better driving directions, but Ken was already in place when I arrived at the library. He was so passionate about his work the interview went smoothly. But I was especially anxious, wondering if I could find the bed and breakfast. I did pretty well for the first two blocks— I only jumped one curb. Then Ken realized I'd taken a wrong turn and guided me the rest of the way. He explained that whenever he came into a new town, he mapped it out in his mind first so he'd know how to focus.

∾

Within six months of Wesley's death, I realized that even though I'd grown to love Tahlequah, it could never be as magical as I wanted it to be. Sometimes my memories there would almost trick me into seeing glimpses of Grandma, Wesley, and the rest of our relatives in the express lane at Safeway or in the parking lot at Wal-Mart. Only the FOR SALE sign in front of Wesley's office finally convinced me that I'd lost them all forever, even in familiar surroundings. I'd still look to the hills beyond Grandma's house and find inspiration, even solace, in the way they'd shielded our family strongholds for so many years. But the time had come. I needed to establish some landmarks of my own.

A few years earlier I'd gotten to know Oklahoma author Billie Letts, whose character Sister Husband in *Where the Heart Is* had once declared, "Home is where your history begins." In my case, volume two of that history would be set in Tulsa, where I'd learn just the sort of person I could be off the road. Commuting had become my standard excuse for not making commitments—either personally or professionally. I could always say "I've got to head for Tulsa," or "I'm on my way to Tahlequah" to avoid difficult decisions. Even after I relocated, I still had trouble embracing life with conviction. When I went to my new Tulsa optometrist for the first time, he flashed two frames of letters before my eyes and asked which looked best to me. I shrugged and said, "I don't know—what do you think?"

On a more profound level, though, distancing myself from Tahlequah gave me the chance to reconsider kinship from a broader perspective. I'd always been fascinated by the way classical mythology had used family relationships to personalize the world and make nature a little less scary. After all, what better way to process an ancient earthquake than by linking it to adultery on Mt. Olympus? Even in modern times, Grandma, who'd taken such pride in her science degree, had explained away my childhood fears of thunder by telling me that God and his son Jesus were just bowling in heaven.

It was that same concept—*family* as a kind of universal equation—that also helped me focus again on the writers and artists I featured on television. In the past, my natural curiosity had almost always put me at ease with our guests, but after Wesley's death I became self-conscious with grief, often losing my concentration in the middle of an interview and repeating myself. Suddenly I was overwhelmed by the whole idea of "live to tape." I'd already learned about words you could never take back, and I was tongue-tied—*heart-tied*—with remorse.

Then I met Arlo Guthrie. We'd arranged to tape a segment with him in an Oklahoma City hotel room. He was in town to accept an award in his father's honor and had agreed to fit us into a tight schedule. Even so, he didn't try to rush us when he arrived and was very patient as we took an extra moment to adjust his lighting and do a microphone check. By that point in my career, I'd rattled off the opening to *Writing Out Loud* hundreds of times, but as I stared across at Arlo, I couldn't get through the first few lines without flubbing, even introducing him at one point as his late father, Woody.

Practically speaking, this meant that we'd have to start over again from the top, and I kept stammering my apologies. Arlo did all he could to level the conversation by telling me how many retakes he'd done his first day on the set of the television series *Byrds of Paradise*. But I was still overly aware of the fact I was talking to Arlo Guthrie, star of *Alice's Restaurant*, son of an American icon, and my questions sounded too scripted for our "real conversations with real people" format.

Initially, I tried not to shortchange Arlo by focusing too much on Woody, but Arlo took the lead himself when he spoke about visiting a music shop that had priced his dad's old driftwood guitar at $250,000. In contrast, Gene Autry's guitar—in pristine condition—had been on sale in the same shop for $50,000. Arlo loved telling the story and became animated with affection as he noted the price difference.

Then he moved on to the more difficult topic of Woody's Huntington's disease and pulled me back into

the interview by demonstrating an important life lesson—
family trumped *celebrity*. In fact, Huntington's, a debilitat-
ing neurological disorder, often passed from generation to
generation, so I was anxious to find out about Arlo's own
health. He'd been spared; he'd inherited his father's talent
but not his infirmity.

> *Wesley used to say I got my musical ability from him—*
> *neither of us could carry a tune.*

I also talked *family* with novelist and poet N. Scott Mo-
maday, whose father Al, a well-known artist, had illustrated
Scott's masterwork, *The Way to Rainy Mountain*. Scott later
became an accomplished artist in his own right, and his
broad-stroked, Kiowa themes are very reminiscent of his father's, though he'd never spent studio time with Al. Instead,
he'd "learned by osmosis" whenever Al's artist friends had
come to visit. As Scott explained the apprenticeship: "I put
my ear to the door and listened." On special days he would
even be invited to join their inner circle for picnics in the
mountains.

> *Wesley once took me to the law office with him, letting*
> *me climb behind his desk and declare, "I object," as my*
> *feet dangled from an oversized chair.*

I know. Arlo's and Scott's *father* stories weren't mine to
savor, but collectively they did become an important frame
of reference for me, especially after I moved to Tulsa and
started sorting through more tricky memories of Wesley.
I'd finally persuaded a veteran psychiatrist to work with me,
though she was in her seventies and not much inclined to
belabor my father's recent passing. It wasn't until I mentioned the Laureate incident that she became intrigued.
"*Estrangement* can be fascinating," she said, and we began

meeting once a month to acknowledge the fact that I was just one Emily Dickinson quote away from being self-indulgent.

I was still holding that last verse in reserve as I prepared to meet Frank McCourt—"I measure every Grief I meet / With narrow, probing, Eyes— / I wonder if It weighs like Mine— / Or has an Easier size." His memoir *Angela's Ashes* had been so heartrending that almost any family loss seemed slight in comparison to what the McCourts had endured. The sequel *'Tis* had just been released, and Frank was going to be our keynote speaker at the Celebration. In fact, I was so preoccupied with the event itself that I almost forgot to meet him at the hotel for what we were already billing as one of those "interviews of a lifetime."

In my haste to introduce myself to this charming man and make up for being so late, I accidentally dropped my microphone through the neck of my blouse and then tried to finesse it through one of the sleeves without attracting too much attention. But it was hopelessly caught on my undergarments, and we didn't have time to reconnect from the base. So as I was asking Frank about his first impressions of Oklahoma, I'd turned my back to him and was unbuttoning my blouse to free the mike. I can only imagine what he was thinking as he asked about my mixed ancestry, part European, part Cherokee. When I did finally pull myself together and faced him again, he helped me laugh through my indiscretion by observing, "If you were to go back in history one hundred years, you wouldn't know whether to defend or attack."

I'd noticed that he was wearing what he explained was a Calladagh ring, which means "I'm yours" in the Irish tradition. The ring, more than just a token to him, clarified his weariness. Off camera he told me he'd been touring all week to promote the new book, hoping to secure the financial future of his family. This was despite being on the best-seller lists, because after losing loved ones to starvation, he didn't feel free to ignore any opportunity. He wanted every guarantee that such a tragedy could never happen again.

The most revealing portion of the interview came when he told how writing *Angela's Ashes* had changed his life personally as well as professionally. He admitted that he'd never realized the intensity of his mother's suffering until he'd started the book and considered her struggles on a deeper level. In retrospect he wished he'd been more considerate of her and not so irritable. Though he emphasized that he hadn't written about his family to put forth a message, he did share the question he'd begun asking himself: "What am I doing now that I might regret?" Up until then, I'd been restless with the question the Wizard of Oz had asked Dorothy—"Who are you?" But I was starting to become haunted in a different way.

∾

Before Billie Letts became an Oprah author, I asked for her business card so we could stay in touch. She seemed embarrassed and explained that she'd been tempted to get some cards, just for the sake of convenience, but she kept imagining what her dad would say. Not that she minded people knowing where she lived. She just didn't want to seem presumptuous. But after Where the Heart Is *became a best seller, I started getting calls at the Center from fans claiming to be Billie's cousins and even her neighbors. That's how convincing her novels could be and the reason rumors have circulated for years that she's lived in several different places all at once. People drive by Billie's house every day without realizing it, because they've found her in her stories. She's become her own next-door neighbor.*

∾

I used to say that I was raised to be delightful, and it's true that Mark, Wesley, all of us to a certain extent, had constantly tried to make up for our shortcomings by being as charming as possible in public settings. Wesley was especially successful. As soon as I started grade school, classmates began pulling me aside to tell me he was taller than he looked. And over the years any number of friends stopped me in the street to declare, "Your father's so funny he ought to be on television." These were just the kinds of illusions we lived with in small towns. We were each other's entertainment, and for the Millers at least, *family* evolved into a performance art.

After Wesley's death I became agreeable to a fault, over-committing myself to avoid any conflict that might reflect the hurt I'd been internalizing for years. That's oversimplifying, I know. Suffice it to say that I was afraid if I let down even for a minute, I might break altogether and find myself in the middle of a *Jerry Springer* episode. Not to mention the fact that I'd become overly gracious at home, too. When Skylar sneezed, I automatically blurted, "God bless you."

I was still visiting with my psychiatrist, Dorothy, and sometimes she would delicately edge a box of Kleenex in my direction, hoping I would eventually open up with her. Certainly she'd asked me all the pointed questions, including the big one: Had I ever considered suicide? "No," I quipped, "homicide's more my style," except it wasn't true, and we both knew it. I'd survived that kind of vast hopelessness after Grandma's death, then again after a romantic breakup. But each time I'd been desperate enough to look beyond the void and relocate myself through celebrity constellations that overreached my loss.

Dorothy and I'd spent several sessions discussing this "work" of mine in relationship to my personal life. In the beginning she'd been suspicious when I'd mentioned various authors, and once she'd even asked me if I'd ever met Virginia Woolf. This was a test, of course, since Woolf had died in 1941. It wasn't until she actually ran across the television show and saw me interviewing Tony Hillerman about his temporary blindness that she became convinced I was, indeed, in a unique job, self-styled to give me a satellite view of the world and my place in it.

Nevertheless, she warned that I was relying on a lonely perspective, and she occasionally broached the subject of antidepressants, which I tried for a few months, then abandoned. Wesley's addictions—and Mark's—had left me too drug-shy to take any medications on a regular basis, but I did finally relent and find relief with antianxiety pills that I could take "as needed."

The "as needed" even referred to my sessions with Dorothy, because she'd been frank from the beginning. She was too old to make a long-term professional commitment to me and had already started to distance herself with this caveat: I was in the midst of an identity crisis of my own— partly due to family, yes—but also due to my inability to write. I had to find a way to get young Marie beyond the carnival.

No wonder I felt such a strong connection to those women who were able to write through the uncertainties in their lives and work on resolutions for all of us. I was especially looking forward to meeting Amy Tan, author of the extraordinary book *The Joy Luck Club*, made to order for me, since it focused almost exclusively on the gaps in mother-daughter relationships.

Initially, I was so excited about signing Amy that I didn't even review the riders in her contract. It wasn't until a week before her arrival that I read the clause noting that "Ms. Tan must have two dogs with her at all times." We'd had some odd requests over the years, but this one stymied me. Where, for God's sake, was I going to find two dogs for Amy Tan? I figured as a last resort, I could use Dash, the puppy I'd just gotten for Skylar, but the vet was already referring to him as "unruly." Finally I checked with Amy's agents, and much to my embarrassment and relief, discovered that she would be bringing her own dogs, medical alert animals trained to signal any health episodes related to her Lyme disease.

As it turned out, Amy brought only one of her Yorkies with her, Lilli, who turned out to be a huge draw in and of herself. In fact, during Amy's press conference, a reporter asked me, "How old is she?" I hesitated a moment, offended on Amy's behalf, but then he quickly explained that, no, he meant Lilli.

For months, I'd been reading that in addition to being a magnificent writer, Amy was also an outstanding presenter, and it was true. She was mesmerizing, artfully weaving together stories about her relationship with her mother that were, in fact, lyrical translations of her mother's broken English—"I think you know little percent of me"—and her broken spirit. Several of us had heard the same confusing banter within our own lives after a major hurt or crisis, and Amy had been able to decipher it for us.

I had equally high expectations for an appearance by Alice Walker, which I hoped would be an important follow-up to the consciousness-raising we'd started with Maya. But as soon as we announced Alice as one of our headliners, I started receiving criticism for featuring too many black women authors. The facts, though, spoke for themselves: we'd showcased literally *hundreds* of writers during the Celebration's four-year history, but only *five* had been black women.

By the way, we'd never gotten similar complaints about our lopsided representation of white male writers, and I looked forward to even more controversy as we worked to make the Celebration truly inclusive. That said, my social commitment, at least to a certain extent, was personally driven. I still regarded any stand I took against discrimination as part of my reconciliation process with Wesley. What had happened to him scared me for all of us—he'd let someone else's prejudice override his own moral values.

Mostly, though, I simply admired Alice Walker. I considered *The Color Purple* one of *the* great novels of American literature, and I always kept it and its message of personal empowerment within easy reach. I'd also become a fan of Alice's sharp literary criticism, particularly her essays on the writings of Flannery O'Connor and Zora Neale Hurston. As far as I was concerned, her efforts to revive interest in Zora's career and to commemorate her grave with a tombstone was one of the all-time great examples of literary generosity.

It's hard to contain that level of admiration. I was so full of anticipation as I rehearsed my "Welcome to Oklahoma speech" that when I actually spotted Alice in the airport lobby, I rushed to embrace her. Clearly the feeling wasn't mutual. She bristled, and I backed off immediately to give her and the woman she was traveling with a little more space while we waited for their luggage. The baggage carousels were painfully slow, and anxious to make amends, I asked Alice about her family. She told me she had a daughter, noting as an aside that she hoped to have grandchildren one day. Then she announced that she didn't like to talk much.

My friend, Norma, and I dropped her off at the hotel as soon as possible and didn't see her again until she rode with us to the Brady. En route we told her about Maya's visit and gave her a brief history of the theater. Her only other comment was that Mercury was in retrograde, which didn't seem to bode well for any of us. Even so, she settled in backstage and waited patiently for Joyce Carol Thomas to formally introduce her. Joyce did a beautiful job highlighting Alice's career, but in many ways it was *The Color Purple* itself that served as Alice's entrée to the community. Her fans, who already considered themselves mutual friends through Celie and Shug, greeted her with enormous enthusiasm.

Though Alice warmed to the crowd, there was still a stiffness about her as she assumed the podium and spoke for a few moments about the turbulent history of the Greenwood riots. Her emotion, however, seemed genuine, and she'd just paused for a moment of quiet reflection when we all heard the banging at the stage door, followed by the announcement, "Pizza's here!" The words echoed throughout the auditorium. One thing about the Brady in those days—you couldn't always count on the discretion of the stagehands, but the theater itself had great acoustics. That was demonstrated all over again, when we got to listen to "Pizza's here" a second time, uttered even more forcefully.

Alice froze for a minute, the ambience shattered, but she finally recovered enough to deliver an impressive talk and then sign books afterward. She'd already made other arrangements to get back to the airport the next morning, so I thanked her for coming, then tried to fax her an official note the next week. I'd meant to rely on the old cop-out line, "I can't tell you what a joy it's been working with you." But faulty technology intervened, jamming the machine, and I saw what I'd accidentally written instead—"I can't tell you what a *job* it's been working with you."

Mercury, the planet of communications, was, indeed, in retrograde, and thankfully Alice never received that reckless message. For, as I've reminded myself many times since, she didn't owe me a heartfelt conversation after she'd already given me a great book. Two great books for that matter. If she hadn't championed Zora's masterpiece, *Their Eyes Were Watching God,* it wouldn't have been reprinted for a whole new generation of readers.

I often think of Alice's relentless search through the Florida underbrush to find Zora's grave and recall that pivotal moment when she claimed to be Zora's niece in order to get more information about her. For me this is an especially comforting notion of kinship—a lineage of admiration that became its own conspiracy against loneliness and grief.

Since I speak so often about family, I'm regularly asked why I haven't married and had children myself. An older friend of mine even wanted to know if I could be gay, which would be an easy explanation in contemporary times. After all, we've mostly outlived the taboos, at least in enlightened circles. What's harder to say these days is that sometimes you wind up single by accident. It can be as capricious as suddenly finding yourself in the company of Maya Angelou or Arlo Guthrie.

And so I trust in the genealogy of shared experience and hope that any bonds I've formed with the like-minded or like-hearted will leave kind thoughts behind for another generation.

∾

When I was driving Isabel Allende, she told such riveting tales about the coup in Chile that Tulsa suddenly seemed foreign to me, and I took an unexpected turn. I'll never know for sure if we were actually going north or south. It's enough to say that I was headed the wrong way—down a one-way street. Isabel told me she'd been there before, not on that particular street, of course, but lost. She explained how women are especially vulnerable, because we're naturally programmed to watch over loved ones in our immediate surroundings. I knew from her book Paula *that she still grieved for her daughter, and so I can only imagine how hard it was for her to look beyond the emptiness and search for helpful signs in the distance.*

∾

In 1999, eighteen years after it was originally published, *Remnants of Glory* was reissued by a regional publisher, and several of my friends got to read the book for the first time. A few had already been able to find older editions on the Internet, but that had been a bittersweet experience for me. As it turned out, many of the original copies that I'd effusively signed to *Patty*s, and *Lucy*s, and *Harry*s had since lost their cachet and been sold to used bookstores. I kept a mental list of all the readers who'd flipped on me, including, most notably, my former next-door neighbor in Tahlequah.

In a way the book had lost some of its allure for me, too, and I sometimes had to puzzle over those dated autographs before I'd be able to acknowledge the flamboyant lettering as mine. Or at least it had been mine once and still was to the extent it was dimly recognizable in the name I kept affixing to contracts, hasty letters, "autographed checks," and the other documents of adult life.

I got that same feeling of detached familiarity when I actually reread the book itself to refresh my memory before writing a preface for the new edition. So much real life had intervened that I found it hard not to intrude as an older writer and steady the younger novelist's hand and heart just a little. The publisher had told me I could make any revisions I felt appropriate, and certainly I was tempted to correct the catfish-with-scales error that had haunted me. More significantly, since I'd become closer in age to my heroine, at least in the earlier sections of the novel, I could now think of several different options for Kate in her later years.

But I didn't believe that I could ever confront old age so boldly again—you have be young to write that brazenly about nursing homes. And there was another important consideration. Making revisions after so long a time could mean getting lost again, more lost than I'd been all those years before in New York. For *Remnants of Glory,* scales and all, had become an important point of reference for where I was at that stage in my life—in Tulsa, Oklahoma, a real-life town just to the west of that make-believe place called Brady.

The more intriguing prospect for me was that the

publisher was also offering me a contract, based on a proposal, for my long-suffering novel-in-progress. Finally I had a legitimate opportunity to follow Dorothy's advice and rescue Marie from that godforsaken carnival, where she'd been detained for so many years that she'd almost become a sideshow herself. But would I be able to actually overcome my writer's block and write again? I wasn't quite sure myself at first and was as surprised as anyone when I brought the novel in on schedule.

In addition to having the ongoing support and friendship of my agent, Mary, who'd never lost faith in me or my writing, two other key factors had worked to my advantage. Knowing that I'd had to meet deadline, imposed by a press so close to home, had intimidated me more than my own self-doubt. Also—and this was a Dorothy contribution—my months in therapy had convinced me that I could no longer evade the truths of my own life, even in fiction.

Family Correspondence was actually two novellas, one focused on Marie, who'd lost her mother to cancer in post–World War II Oklahoma; the other centered on Marie's daughter, Nora, who'd lost Marie in a mysterious car accident. This "mystery" wasn't the kind of intrigue I'd learned to expect in some of my favorite suspense novels by P. D. James and Elizabeth George. Instead it emphasized those everyday misunderstandings that made even the closest of relatives seem inscrutable to each other.

The biggest risk I took was trying to write a transitional scene between the two stories that bridged the gap, so to speak. I also used letters from other characters between the various chapters, my idea being that they would speak to the broader reach of community, that "bigger than family correspondence." But readers had a mixed reaction to the format. Some second-guessed my decision to leave certain questions unanswered, and I could actually relate to their frustrations. I'd lived with them myself as I'd tried to piece together the life of my own mother. That's why the vagaries had seemed more sincere to me.

And with this second book, I wasn't equivocating—it was highly autobiographical. Even more so structurally than thematically. I hadn't realized that until I'd hit an impasse one day and recalled all the troubles I'd had writing transitions for *Remnants*. In fact, the first person quotes I'd finally used to tie that story together were very similar to the letters I'd included in the new novel. But the letters weren't just literary devices. They were life strategies, some of the same tricky segues I'd always relied on to get beyond those empty chairs Mother could have filled at birthday parties, graduations—and book signings.

I'd had several recurring dreams about Mother over the years. In one, she'd suddenly awaken after being in an extended coma, which Wesley had kept secret from us because her prognosis had been so poor. Naturally I'd be elated to hear such news, except for the Wesley part, and would rush to the hospital, overwhelmed with everything I'd always wanted to tell her. Only a nurse would be blocking the door, telling me, "You can't do this to your mother. If you try to catch her up on all that's happened, it's going to kill her." That's how the dream always left off, until I stopped having it altogether—right after *Family Correspondence* was published. I'd searched and searched for Mother within the pages of that story, but after I wrote the ending, she was gone forever, spent from my imagination, just like Grandma had tried to tell me.

The book also helped me find closure to the romance I'd been hoping would somehow come to life again, despite mutual feelings of betrayal. Admittedly I've tried to evade this subject, even within these pages, for once you lose someone to death, it's hard to believe that anything less powerful can separate you from people who've meant so much to you. I think it's enough to say that when Nora reminded her former lover that he'd promised to love her forever, he responded by telling her, "And for a while, honey, I did." This was my admission that Wesley had been right—I'd spent too much time trying to reclaim the past, and I finally did let go of most of my old grievances, except for my anger toward him.

But *Family Correspondence* was much more than just a psychological breakthrough. Like the first incarnation of *Remnants of Glory,* it became my literal "letter of transit," a way for me to venture out again as a writer and live beyond the boundaries I'd set for myself. I was even discovering a global network. A book club in Kyoto, Japan, had learned about both novels on the Internet and had chosen them as reading selections. Though I didn't get to accept the club's invitation to visit Kyoto, I loved the idea that readers so many miles away were relating to the stories, and I saved all the pictures, cards, and e-mails they sent on a regular basis.

"Why can't Americans use books to bond like this?" I'd say rather smugly as Jonathan pored over the latest Harry Potter title. I'd asked him rather pointedly if he thought anyone, a nephew even, might stay up all night reading one of my novels, and he'd shrugged, pointing to my Japanese friends as a possibility. I kept a group photo of all ten club members in my office, and I'd bought a red lotus water-color print for the house as an ongoing reminder of my most devoted fans. One had even sent an e-mail saying, "I hoping to keep in touch with each other for long."

For the most part, though, I was still regarded as a re-gional novelist, and I began to sympathize more and more with other aspiring writers who were trying to promote their work. That's why, for the first time in the history of *Writing Out Loud,* I finally relented and featured a guest whose work I couldn't appreciate. Friends had been pres-suring me for weeks to interview the local poet because he was such a nice guy, but I'd been embarrassed by the show.

The man had read relentlessly from a pamphlet he'd put together of awkwardly rhymed farm humor.

Writer and radio commentator Connie Cronley was still teasing me about the program when we drove to Oklahoma City for a joint signing the Saturday after the broadcast. During the event, a woman rushed over to our table, noted she was a regular viewer of *Writing Out Loud*, and congratulated me on having a new book available. Elated, I was already autographing a copy for her when she patted my hand gently, then explained that she was really hoping to get in touch with the "farm poet," whose work, she said, had moved her deeply. In passing, she promised she'd "peruse" my book some other time.

Another signing, this time in Wichita with author John Wooley, was even more challenging. After driving for over five hours, John and I found ourselves stationed at a table in front of a chain store restroom, listening as a disgruntled clerk spent the entire afternoon sharing her personal traumas. So we took turns. John excused himself during the story of a cousin's kidney transplant, and I grabbed a break during the adoption-gone-bad monologue. We even had to spell each other during the ride home, trading personal anecdotes to distract us from the end result—we hadn't sold a single book between us.

I'd also returned to a disturbing e-mail exchange, breaking news from Japan. Due to unspecified rifts, the Kyoto book club had permanently disbanded, and the readers were all going their separate ways. Translation: *sayonara.*

By far the two highlights of my author travels were the trips I made to Los Angeles to visit Betsy Hailey and speak at the literary luncheons she sponsored for a women's care group. During the first visit, I was appearing with television commentator/newspaper columnist Lee Cullum. Lee, Betsy, and I had a wonderful time touring Los Angeles. We spent one morning with Betsy's daughter Kendall at the

Huntington Museum and admired a Bloomsbury exhibit that showcased the works of Vanessa Bell, Duncan Grant, and their clique of literary artists. Later we settled in at Betsy's, and as we discussed writing and life, I felt that same sense of belonging, Bloomsbury light, that I'd experienced as a younger writer in New York.

So I was delighted to accept when Betsy invited me to appear before the same group again the next year—this time as part of an ensemble presentation with Earl Hamner and Ronnie Claire Edwards. She was billing us as "Earl Hamner and the Dixie Chicks" and had also helped set up a book signing for us at an independent bookstore the night before the luncheon. As soon as we arrived for the signing, we casually mentioned to Ronnie Claire that we'd seen Julie Andrews and her husband, Blake Edwards, across the street at a restaurant. Though Ronnie Claire was as gracious as always, she quickly excused herself, motioned to her young protégé, and seemed to whisper some sort of instructions. It wasn't until I was standing at the podium and saw Julie Andrews sitting a little nervously in the back row that I made the connection.

The luncheon itself was exhilarating—with several Hollywood personalities in attendance. Betsy had already pointed out Jayne Meadows to me, reminding me that she had recently lost her husband, Steve Allen. I'd also spotted Barbara Rush and was suddenly so intimidated that I wasn't able to relax until Earl and Ronnie Claire did such wonderful presentations that all I had to do was take advantage of the goodwill they had generated.

Afterwards, I was thrilled when Jayne approached me and asked me to autograph a copy of *Family Correspondence.* As I was signing her book, she told me how sorry she was I'd had to see her in such a light. I nodded and passed along my condolences, noting how much I'd admired her husband. But she was shaking her head, explaining, "No, this light," as she raised her arms expansively to call my attention to a row of high intensity overhead lamps. She was an artist, after all, and understood the importance of nuances. Later, as I had a chance to reflect, not just on what she said, but also on my own experiences, I understood what she meant. Life was complicated enough without putting too fine an illumination on it. That's why I kept looking to those who cast larger shadows.

∾

After people started reading Remnants *again, they sometimes asked if I'd lost track of Kate's sister in the story, and I'd have to explain that I'd mentioned her fate in the prologue. But the book did become more focused on Kate than her extended family as she fought to establish her own identity. It's been much the same with Mark and me. To locate each other these days, we have to start at the very beginning. I have a Kodak snapshot, though, that always helps me find a way back to him. He's five and posing with our one-eyed dog Tuffy, his hand discreetly covering Tuffy's infirmity. That's our bond now—we're the only ones still left who realize what was missing.*

∾

When I got back to Oklahoma, I tried to hold on to the sense of community I'd experienced at Betsy's and reinvest it in the Celebration of Books, which had gradually taken on the feel of a big, splashy reunion. Many writers came more than once, and part of the event's appeal was getting to catch up on a regular basis with old friends like novelists Rilla Askew, Linda Phillips, and Edward Swift.

So even if the Celebration was a manifestation of what was missing in my life, it had also begun generating its own agenda, as writers started reaching out to other writers and inviting them to attend. I would never have guessed, for instance, when I first interviewed novelist/cartoonist Doug Marlette that he would later move to Tulsa from North Carolina, then convince the legendary Pat Conroy to be one of our headliners. Pat, by the way, was a huge fan of Earl Hamner's, so that Celebration we had the most balanced fictional view of family in the history of our event—*The Waltons Meet the Great Santini.*

In addition to doing the Celebration, I'd also started hosting stand-alone events for special occasions. One year we presented an honorary award to actress Shirley Jones, who'd starred in the movie musical *Oklahoma,* based on *Green Grow the Lilacs* by Oklahoma playwright Lynn Riggs. Initially Shirley was concerned that we might expect her to ride in a surrey, since she'd regularly been called upon to commemorate her portrayal of Laurey in that way. Apparently almost every city she visited claimed to own the original surrey from the film.

Though we did, indeed, have access to an *original* surrey, we ordered her an oversized limo instead, and I rode with her to the banquet so we could review the evening's agenda. En route she pulled out her wallet to show me pictures of her children and grandchildren, including her celebrity offspring, Patrick, Shaun, and Ryan, and stepson David Cassidy. They were all so attractive that I was reminded of the glossy movie star photos that always came in bargain billfolds, except these people, recognizable to so many of us, were her actual relatives. I asked her then what other profession she would have chosen if she hadn't been in show business, singing with Gordon McCrae and playing her stepson's real mother on *The Partridge Family.*

Of course, I'd been somewhat emboldened by sparkles in the limo ceiling—the illusion of stars—and was looking to her as the embodiment of my own early aspirations and needs. But she'd trafficked in expectations her whole career and positioned herself with camera perfect posture, absorbing a succession of speed bumps, to tell me that she would have been a veterinarian.

The Center also sponsored the national book launch for Elmore Leonard's novel *The Hot Kid*, which was set in Oklahoma. We were going to do a television program with Elmore, too, and I visited with the crew the morning of the event to make sure everything was in order. I was just leaving for lunch and my first meeting with Elmore, when I tripped and slid under my car. Thankfully, Gary was close at hand and helped me get behind the wheel so I could drive on to the restaurant. I was even able to hobble inside before any of the other guests arrived, and I successfully hid my discomfort throughout our meal. But once I stood to excuse myself, I realized the extent of my injury—I'd broken my foot.

Still, I wasn't about to give up my one shot at a two-part interview with Elmore, so Gary devised a plan. We were taping in the historic Mayo Hotel, and he angled our chairs in such a way that I could be seen only from the waist up, which meant the viewing audience would never know that all the while I was visiting with Elmore—both of us surrounded by gold filigree—my foot was soaking in a bucket of ice.

My only concern was that I didn't want Elmore to feel compromised by our unconventional setup. But I needn't have worried. He couldn't have been more solicitous, offering me a piece of the hard candy he always carried in his jacket pocket and trying not to focus too much on my foot. By the time we'd gotten halfway through the interview, it was almost as if my predicament had become a secret we shared, and he seemed to be even more forthcoming. Like so many great writers, he understood *broken*.

Another special event I was particularly looking forward to was what we were labeling generically as *An Evening with Dave Barry.* I'd been listening to Dave one Sunday on C-Span 2, shortly after 9/11, and had found myself laughing for the first time in weeks. I'd determined then that, if it were at all possible, I wanted to bring him to Tulsa. As it turned out, his assistant was from Oklahoma, which might have influenced him a little, and he accepted our invitation, thrilling not only me, but also hundreds of other devoted fans. In fact we had so many calls from people wanting to meet with him personally, I asked for added security and limited backstage access to the four of us who'd be appearing on stage that evening.

As per my instructions, the security guards at the Tulsa Performing Arts Center didn't take any risks and even questioned Dave and me before leading us back to the green-room. The university president was already waiting for us, and I also saw Clifton Taulbert, who was going to be introducing Dave. Cliff was visiting with an older man I didn't recognize, but they seemed to be carrying on a spirited conversation, so I just assumed the stranger was one of Cliff's many business associates. It was only after I got a moment alone with Cliff to brief him on the program that I asked about his guest. "Why, that's Dave's father," he said. "He just happened to come early."

"Dave's father is dead," I whispered, telling Cliff to keep the man occupied until I got security to escort him outside.

The man left without incident, and Dave, unruffled, went on to give a hilarious performance, even working in some pointed satire, including his own take on the lyrics to *Oklahoma.* I was keeping watch from backstage and would occasionally peek from behind the curtain to look into the audience. That's when I saw him, "Dave Barry's father," who was sitting next to an exact clone on the front row and laughing uproariously.

I sent for the guard, who assured me that "the twins," as he called them, were just celebrity enthusiasts and totally harmless. While the one brother had been backstage with us, the other brother had been in the lobby, pretending to be Anthony Hopkins traveling incognito. People had actually lined up to get "Anthony's" autograph, even though the man hadn't resembled Hopkins in the slightest. But I wasn't surprised. I knew as well as anyone that *celebrity* was in the eye of the beholder, particularly during troubled times; we even expected our imposters to sign off on the deception.

What disturbed me even more than the twins themselves was the backstage security breach, a reminder to all of us that, despite our many precautions, all sorts of intruders, some transfigured as memories, were just waiting to catch us unawares.

∾

After my friend Norma and I left a local lecture hall, we walked for ten minutes before we realized we'd been following each other and getting nowhere. As it turned out, neither of us could remember where we'd parked until we started calculating our way together. Norma had become like a second mother to me, but sometimes she'd lose patience with my naiveté. Once, when I told her that I was trying to do the right thing at work, she explained, "Honey, you don't understand. I'm not trying to get you to do the right thing. I'm trying to get you to be manipulative and devious."

∾

One blustery March day, for reasons that weren't really clear to me at first, I came home disconsolate. That's the only way I know to describe the sense of despair and grief I suddenly felt as my mind started overloading with images of Wesley. It wasn't until I saw the 28th circled on my calendar that I remembered his birthday and realized that, despite our painful history together, I couldn't bear losing him completely. In the end, choosing *mercy* over *justice* was just that simple.

That's not to say that I would ever be able to condone many of his actions, particularly his failure to protect me from my stepmother because *he had wanted to avoid the gossip.* For even though I'd come to understand the role small-town pressures might have played, I couldn't excuse that kind of superficial disregard for a child who'd depended on him. In fact I still wasn't sure he was being totally honest with either of us when he'd settled on that explanation.

All I could know for certain was that we'd waited too late to make peace in the traditional ways—with heartfelt confessions and loving embraces. But I did have one consolation: I was convinced that he'd foreseen this change in me, even from his hospital bed, when he'd given up hope of a more immediate reconciliation. I'm not suggesting he had any kind of extended spiritual vision, but he understood human nature—not at its best, because that kind of idealism was for amateurs who folded before real-life juries. His secret was that he understood human nature *after* it had already been compromised.

I suppose that's why my most comforting memories of our relationship don't focus on poignant gift exchanges or father-daughter pep talks. What I actually miss most about him are the verbal battles, sometimes harsh, that speak not so much to our disagreements, as to our willingness to set aside any pretenses between us. Because sometimes, if genuine warmth isn't possible, there can be a special closeness, even respect, that comes from learning not to expect too much.

So I began savoring some of our old disputes—with their not-so-subtle undertones. "You're going to kill both of us, you know," he'd said, when I'd been taking him from Tahlequah to Tulsa for his radiation treatments. "A man out at the Ford dealership told me just the other day that you were the worst driver of any of us—never coming to a complete stop, speeding through the caution lights."

We'd just passed a roadside memorial, one of those makeshift crosses with artificial flowers that marked the site of a fatal accident. This one was new, but we'd see more before the day was over, because SH 82 was a risky highway even for happy families.

"And you better slow down for that dog," he'd said. "Sometimes cows can get loose, too. If you hit a cow, if you hit a dog, or even a wet patch . . ."

The *ifs* had gone on and on, because he'd just lost a friend to the same illness he was battling himself, and we'd both silently acknowledged the harsher implications of the highway we were traveling. It was an alternate route, the one you took when Steinbeck's "Mother Road" with its promise of prosperity didn't go far enough, and you finally saw how bare the overall prospects could be.

Or not. Wesley's own prognosis had been so good that I'd called him Buster and then announced that we were stopping for ice cream on the way home, whether it made us late or not. That had lightened the mood for both of us, and we'd even become strangely playful then, waving to other travelers, some of whom honked back at us, as if to acknowledge our shared journey and wish us well.

Through the years these same kinds of shared observances or rites of passage seemed to carry over to my work, particularly *Writing Out Loud*, which was based on the premise that we were literally catching lives in motion, so we could hold onto them a little longer, maybe even forever.

Some of our guests had triumphed over major illnesses and continued to inspire us with their hopeful messages. Wilma Mankiller, former principal chief of the Cherokees, is a prime example. By the time Wilma first appeared on our program, she'd survived lymphoma, myasthenia gravis, severe kidney disease, and breast cancer with such grace that she had an unmistakable presence about her that was calming, not just for me but also for our audience. As one viewer put it, she made you want to reach out and touch the television.

Wilma had been fighting off a cold that day, which must have seemed trivial in comparison to the other illnesses she'd overcome, but I was still struck by her quiet resistance to it. Though she wore her coat during our visit and kept a single tissue in hand, she tolerated her symptoms without letting them alter her demeanor or her forthright answers. She confirmed that she'd relied on both conventional and Cherokee medicine—and that she supported stem cell research.

Another guest, movie critic Joel Siegel, had also been diagnosed with cancer, though he acknowledged that his prognosis was uncertain. The father of a young son, Dylan, he was focused on being a devoted parent and had even written a book, *Lessons for Dylan,* so the boy would have a chance to know his father if Joel didn't survive. Though Joel had met many of the world's most glamorous celebrities and told about his visit with Nicole Kidman and Tom Cruise, it was clear that Dylan was the major star in his life.

We were taping the interview with Joel in a hotel room, and so even though we were speaking to a larger audience, our conversation seemed to take on the trappings of the room itself and become more personal after we wrapped the show. My dear friend, singer Debbie Campbell, a regular on our program, was dying of cancer, and Joel visited with me about ways I could be more supportive.

One of our most haunting and moving guests, Jack Eisner, had suffered in a different way. He was a Holocaust survivor, who'd written and spoken extensively about his experiences as a teenager in Auschwitz. Although he and his mother were the only members of his family who'd lived through the carnage, he was a remarkably gentle man, who kept smiling over at his wife throughout the interview. Not that he appeared the least bit anxious; he just seemed to like reminding himself that she was only a few feet away.

Shortly after our interview, Jack died of cancer, a disease that also went on to claim the lives of Joel Siegel and Debbie Campbell. Occasionally, I rewatch their interviews, but not to be maudlin. It's my way of setting up those roadside markers, if you will, and commemorating their journeys.

I'd also gotten to visit with Shelby Foote shortly before his death, but because of his advanced age, his passing wasn't unexpected, and we approached the program as a retrospective, which seemed to suit Shelby just fine. He'd liked going on record about his career, especially after discovering that I was a loyal Democrat, which mattered more to him than any of my literary credentials. A few weeks after we broadcast the show, someone, claiming to be a congressional investigator, left a voice mail for me wanting any contact information I had for Shelby, but I never returned the call. We really were kindred political spirits.

Since I'm not religious, at least according to traditional definitions, these successive losses, some more personal than others, often left me greedy for sacred moments. That was the case on July 10, 2007, when I met a friend for lunch so we could celebrate her upcoming birthday and "reverence life." I even ignored my cell phone, more persistent than usual, to order wine and ritualize all the classic clichés about making the most out the time we'd been allotted— and not just for lunch. We were both feeling shortchanged by the progression of years.

It wasn't until I was on my way back to the office that I finally checked my messages and learned that Doug Marlette, returning from his father's funeral, had been killed in a freak auto accident in Mississippi. At first I had trouble processing the news. I'd never met anyone as animated as Doug, and he was so vividly alive in my imagination I became convinced that someone had made a mistake. But the

Tulsa World, where'd he been the political cartoonist for a little over a year, confirmed the tragedy.

After Doug's move to Tulsa, our visits had crossed boundaries, too, covering almost every topic imaginable—Harper Lee, favorite films, sweet tea, our pets, politics. So there were many roads that brought him into my life. Only one road took him away. The day after his accident, Suzanne O'Brien, Darcy's widow, called to tell me that she'd lost a friend on the very same highway during another rainstorm, and it's tempting to resort to words like *treacherous*. But the routes we travel are never easy, and it somehow diminishes the greater journey to focus on the hazards that seem to await all of us. Better to look forward to those unexpected intersections where someone like Doug or Joel or even Wesley could be waiting to point us in a new direction.

∽

My cousin Isabel's father-in-law owned a huge tract of land on the edge of Tahlequah that used to terrify me with its wildness. I could just imagine getting lost amid the snakes and polecats lurking in the waist-high brush. Sometimes the creatures actually sought me out and crept into my nightmares. But the grandfather, a former barber, was enterprising and decided to subdivide the property into a housing addition, naming the streets after his grandchildren. For a time I even lived on Donn Avenue and marveled at how a place that had once been so fearsome for me had become a safe haven of familiarity.

∽

Even though I no longer lived in Tahlequah, it remained an important touchstone in my life. Lori and I often noted the irony: I didn't learn to appreciate Tahlequah until I moved to Tulsa. She and I continued to visit by phone almost every day, so it wasn't as if I felt all that far removed from local happenings. Basically I still knew what the hairdressers knew, which meant I was up-to-speed on all the latest gossip—both on and off Main Street.

Occasionally I still dreamed of really stretching my boundaries and settling in New York or Los Angeles. Mostly though, I was content just to enjoy my work in Tulsa and travel when I could. The majority of my trips were book-driven, since I'd met so many authors through the years who regularly invited me to visit. But I continued to traffic in show business, too, and as soon as Streisand announced her long-awaited concert tour—this time with *Il Divo*—I convinced Lori to go to Vegas with me.

This was the first Vegas outing for both of us, and we saw all the world's most famous attractions—only without the provenance. The Eiffel Tower apart from Paris was just another spectacle, albeit an impressive one. That's not to say that we didn't indulge ourselves as we crossed the strip from the Great Pyramid to the Grand Canals. But for us, Streisand was what made the trip credible. I'd been a fan for years, and in many ways, she'd become the voice of my discontent. I'd played "Gotta Move" over and over as a teen-ager to lash out at small-town life and had gotten through two broken engagements listening to "Free Again," "Cry Me a River," and "The Way We Were."

Since the show was a sellout, we arrived at the arena a little early just to secure our seats and were approached almost immediately by a woman who looked vaguely familiar. She greeted me by name and explained that she was from Tulsa and a regular attendee at the Celebration of Books. We all took note of the coincidence. Just imagine—running into each other in a crowd of fifteen thousand people that also included such luminaries as Billie Jean King and Rosie O'Donnell.

We had a similar experience the next day while we were waiting to board at the Vegas airport. Though we'd had a great trip, we were restless in line, so eager to get home that we basically ignored the other passengers to focus instead on our memories of the concert. Streisand had been in great voice, and as middle-aged women, we especially applauded her decision to take off her heels to get through the encores. I was still humming "Happy Days Are Here Again," twisting in my own shoes, when Lori nudged me and pointed to an attractive woman standing in front of us. "Isn't that Mary Baker?" she asked, and as if on cue Mary turned around to greet us. We'd gone through public school together but hadn't seen each other in years. As it turned out, she and her husband were Streisand fans, too.

Later, after we'd gotten settled in our seats and ordered drinks, Lori smiled and said, "She really looked good, didn't she?" At first I thought she was referring to Barbra, whom I'd just proclaimed as the greatest female singer of all time, but then I understood. She meant Mary, of course, who seemed even more connected to us once we discovered her outside of Tahlequah.

That's when I began to value these encounters as more than just serendipity. Mary and the woman we'd met earlier *did* have provenance—at least for us personally. For we shared a common point of origin, which felt almost sacred in an everyday sort of way. It's what made us familiar to each other, even amid the distractions of Vegas. As a teenager I'd failed to reach out to my cousin at Six Flags, too timid to believe I could find someone close so far away. But once you've traveled enough to admit your feet are weary, you're better able to embrace what you *think* you recognize, even at the risk of strangeness.

The pilot had announced that we were flying at an altitude of 35,000 feet and pointed out the Grand Canyon. The view was stunning, and I spent the rest of the trip recalling other highpoints in my life—the professional dreams I'd realized, the well-known people I'd gotten to meet. It wasn't until we prepared to land that I began to appreciate the simple joy of our descent—those gentle downward circles gradually bringing Tulsa into sharper focus so I could recover my bearings. Jonathan, I knew, was to the south, my dear friend Judy and her family to the east. Other friends and relatives were out west and north. Over time the coordinates were likely to change—that was the nature of life. Still, what a liberating concept, coming after so many years, to think that if I did get lost again, my heart would guide me.

Acknowledgments

My loving appreciation goes to Mary Evans, aka Neva Ramsey, for rescuing *Remnants of Glory* from the slush pile all those years ago and championing my dreams. No one could have asked for a more devoted agent, mentor, and friend.

Many of my other friends and relatives are included in the memoir itself, so I literally can't think of my life without them, but I especially want to thank Judy Hubble, Linda Heflebower, Sherry Huber, and Billie Letts for their support and encouragement.

I'm also indebted to the kindness and professionalism of publisher John Drayton, who sifted through my ideas and found a title for these remembrances, and to Dennis Letts, who thought of the book before I did.

When I was a young writer, the critics caught me writing about catfish with scales—the reason I'm truly beholden to my editors, Steven Baker and Jo Ann Reece, for being so meticulous, and to authors Rilla Askew, Linda Phillips, Michael Wallis, and John Wooley for being such sensitive, insightful readers.

I should note, too, that excerpts from "Legends" originally appeared in *Oklahoma Today*, and I'm grateful to editor-in-chief Louisa McCune for believing in me enough to challenge me with a deadline.

As a teacher, I've tried to challenge my students in that same way, but mostly they have inspired me. I'm proud of all of them, beginning with Stephani Cae Freeman, who was in one of my very first classes and taught *me* through her own good example.

Another great pleasure of my career has been the opportunity to work with two superb directors and creative partners on *Writing Out Loud*, Dale McKinney at Rogers State

University and Gary Johns at Oklahoma State University. Their patience even exceeds their artistry.

And I owe John Cummings of the Claremore Police Department more than I can say for his dedication and valor during such unsettling times.